LEGAL REASONING

The common law, which is made by courts, consists of rules that govern relations between individuals, such as torts (the law of private wrongs) and contracts. *Legal Reasoning* explains and analyzes the modes of reasoning utilized by the courts in making and applying common law rules. These modes include reasoning from binding precedents (prior cases that are binding on the deciding court); reasoning from authoritative although not binding sources, such as leading treatises; reasoning from analogy; reasoning from propositions of morality, policy, and experience; reasoning from hypotheticals; making exceptions; drawing distinctions; and overruling. The book further examines and explains the roles of logic, deduction, and good judgment in legal reasoning. With accessible prose and full descriptions of illustrative cases, this book is a valuable resource for anyone who wishes to get a hands-on grasp of legal reasoning.

Melvin A. Eisenberg is Jesse H. Choper Professor of Law Emeritus, University of California, Berkeley Law School. He is the author of The Nature of the Common Law and Foundational Principles of Contract Law.

.

Legal Reasoning

Melvin A. Eisenberg
University of California, Berkeley

CAMBRIDGE
UNIVERSITY PRESS

CAMBRIDGE
UNIVERSITY PRESS

University Printing House, Cambridge CB2 8BS, United Kingdom

One Liberty Plaza, 20th Floor, New York, NY 10006, USA

477 Williamstown Road, Port Melbourne, VIC 3207, Australia

314–321, 3rd Floor, Plot 3, Splendor Forum, Jasola District Centre,
New Delhi – 110025, India

103 Penang Road, #05–06/07, Visioncrest Commercial, Singapore 238467

Cambridge University Press is part of the University of Cambridge.

It furthers the University's mission by disseminating knowledge in the pursuit of
education, learning, and research at the highest international levels of excellence.

www.cambridge.org
Information on this title: www.cambridge.org/9781009162524
DOI: 10.1017/9781009162517

© Melvin A. Eisenberg 2022

First published 2022

A catalogue record for this publication is available from the British Library.

ISBN 978-1-009-16252-4 Hardback
ISBN 978-1-009-16250-0 Paperback

Cambridge University Press has no responsibility for the persistence or accuracy of
URLs for external or third-party internet websites referred to in this publication
and does not guarantee that any content on such websites is, or will remain,
accurate or appropriate.

To Helen

CONTENTS

PREFACE

This preface provides an overture to the chapters of this book.

Chapter 1. An Introduction to the Common Law. One of two legal systems prevails in most developed economies: common law or civil law. In civil law systems the law is found in statutes, executive decrees, and Civil Codes – codifications of the law of obligations, property, and family. In common law systems public law, which concerns such matters as the organization of government, is made by legislatures and administrative agencies while private law, which concerns such matters as the relationship between individuals, is largely made by the courts. The purpose of this book is to explain and analyze legal reasoning in the common law.

Chapter 2. Rule-Based Legal Reasoning. Common law courts have two functions: resolving disputes according to legal rules and making legal rules. A common law rule is a relatively specific legal norm, established by the courts, that requires persons to act or not act in a specified way; enables or disables specified types of arrangements, such as contracts, and dispositions, such as wills, or specifies remedies for designated wrongs. Reasoning in the common law is almost entirely rule-based – that is, based on the application of legal rules to the facts of the case to be decided. Legal reasoning in the common law is occasionally but infrequently analogy-based and is almost never similarity-based.

Chapter 3. Stare Decisis. The foundation of rule-based reasoning in the common law is the principle of stare decisis, a Latin phrase which means to stand by things decided. Under the principle of stare decisis when a court decides a case that is governed by a rule established in a precedent – a prior case decided by a superior court or by the deciding court itself – the deciding court must apply that rule, subject to the limits of the principle. Without stare decisis there would be no common law: precedents would be persuasive but not binding. But there are a number of limits on this principle. The most important limit is that in most areas of the common law if a rule established in a precedent is not even substantially congruent with social morality and social policy the courts can and frequently will overrule it.

Chapter 4. What Rule a Precedent Establishes. Because the common law consists largely of rules established in precedents the question arises, how it is determined what rule a precedent establishes? The answer is that the rule a precedent establishes is the rule that the court stated governed the case before it. This rule is known as the holding of the case. Statements in a precedent about the law other than the holding are known as dicta. Holdings establish binding legal rules. Dicta are not binding but they are often influential.

Chapter 5. Authoritative Rules. The most prominent type of rules in common law reasoning are rules established in legally binding precedents. The next most prominent types are authoritative although not legally binding rules. These are rules that courts adhere to not because after careful consideration they conclude it is the best possible rule, but because it was adopted in a source, such as a prominent legal treatise, to which the courts give deference.

Chapter 6. Social Propositions. The common law is based on doctrinal and social propositions. Doctrinal propositions are propositions that purport to state legal rules and are found in sources that in the view of the legal profession – judges, practicing lawyers, and legal academics – state legal doctrine. Social propositions are moral, policy, and experiential propositions. The two types of propositions do different work. Doctrinal propositions are legal rules. Social propositions are the reasons for legal rules. The moral propositions that count in common law reasoning are moral propositions that are rooted in aspirations for the community as a whole and have substantial support in the community. The policy propositions that count in common law reasoning are policy propositions that have substantial support in the community, or in the absence of explicit support, can fairly be believed would have such support if the community addressed the policy issues involved.

Chapter 7. Rules, Principles, and Standards. Legal norms can be divided into rules, principles, and standards. Legal rules are relatively specific legal norms that require persons to act or not act in specified ways, enable or disable specified arrangements or dispositions, or set remedies for specified wrongs. Legal principles are relatively general legal norms. Legal standards take several forms. One form is a general legal norm. This form does not significantly differ from a legal principle. The most significant type of legal standard consists of legal rules that are not applicable when they are adopted because they are designed to be further elaborated, often by an administrative agency, when more thought or more information has been developed concerning the way in which the rule should be elaborated.

Chapter 8. The Malleability of Common Law Rules. Legal rules are either canonical or malleable. A canonical rule is fixed. It may not be expressed in different ways, cannot evolve, and cannot be made subject to exceptions. Statutes are the paradigm form of canonical rules. In contrast a malleable rule can be expressed in different ways, can evolve, and can be made subject to exceptions. Common law rules are the paradigm form of malleable rules. They can be expressed in different ways, can evolve, and can be made subject to exceptions.

Chapter 9. Exceptions and Distinctions. A court faced with an established legal rule that seems applicable to the case to be decided has several choices. The court can and usually will apply the established rule. Or the court can make an exception to the established rule or draw a distinction between the established rule and the case to be decided. Exceptions and distinctions fall into several categories. They may be fact-based, that is, based on a material difference between the facts of the precedent that adopted the established rule and the facts of the case to be decided. They may be rule-based, that is, based a conclusion that an established rule that plausibly applies to the case to be decided does not do so when the applicability of the rule is more carefully considered. They may be socially based, that is, based on a conclusion that the social propositions that underlie the established rule do not apply to the case to be decided, or that the case to be decided involves social propositions that were not applicable to the established rule. Alternatively, the court can hive off a new rule to govern a subclass of the cases to which the established rule applies. In that case the established rule and the hived-off rule live side-by-side. Finally, the court can overrule the established rule.

Chapter 10. Analogy-Based Legal Reasoning. Courts occasionally reason from analogy rather than by rule. In most fields outside law reasoning by analogy is based on a similarity between the characteristics of a given state of affairs or state of facts and the characteristics a new state of affairs or state of facts. Law, however, is based not on characteristics but on rules. Accordingly, when a court reasons from analogy usually the analogy is to rules rather than to similar cases. In rule-based analogical reasoning a court begins with an established rule that is not literally applicable to the case to be decided, and extends that rule to cover the case to be decided on the ground that the established rule and the case to be decided cannot be meaningfully distinguished as a matter of social propositions. Courts seldom reason by analogy because a court would never reason by analogy when an established rule governs the case to be decided and the common law is rich with established rules.

Chapter 11. Logic, Deduction, and Good Judgment. Logic. There are a great many schools of formal logic, but in law the term logic is usually used to mean sound reasoning rather than reasoning that satisfies the criteria of formal logic. *Deduction* is a reasoning process in which a conclusion necessarily follows from stated premises. Deduction normally takes the form of a syllogism. A syllogism consists of a general statement, known as a major premise (as in, All men are mortal), a specific statement, known as a minor premise (as in, Socrates is a man), and a conclusion that necessarily follows from the two premises (as in, Socrates is mortal). But as the great English legal philosopher H. L.A. Hart pointed out, "deductive reasoning, which for generations has been cherished as the very perfection of human reasoning, cannot serve as a model . . . for what judges should do in bringing cases under general rules." *Good judgment.* In contrast to formal logic and deduction, good judgment is an important element of legal reasoning. Good judgment consists of the ability to make sound and well-rooted decisions based on established legal rules and principles, together with a breadth of vision and an understanding of how the law can advance the common good. Good judges have good judgment. Great judges have excellent judgment.

Chapter 12. Reasoning from Hypotheticals. This chapter analyzes reasoning from hypotheticals. The term hypothetical means a fact that is assumed rather than actual. The term reasoning from hypotheticals means a scenario consisting of hypotheticals. Reasoning from hypotheticals is employed throughout the law – in adjudication, in oral arguments, and in law school teaching. Chapter 12 explores and illustrates the modes of reasoning from hypotheticals in the common law. In the most important mode a court employs reasoning from hypotheticals to view the case to be decided in a broader form to help decide the case.

Chapter 13. Overruling. This chapter concerns overruling, which occurs when a court overturns – abolishes –a rule established in binding precedents. Overruling can be explicit or implicit. Explicit overruling occurs when a court explicitly abolishes an established rule and replace it with the opposite rule. Implicit overruling occurs when a court undoes a rule but does not purport to do so. At first glance overruling may seem inconsistent with the principle of stare decisis. In fact it isn't, because stare decisis is subject to several exceptions, the most important of which is that if a rule established in precedents is not even substantially congruent with social propositions it can be overruled. Furthermore, overruling is itself governed by a principle: a common law rule should be overruled if it is not even substantially congruent with social propositions, is inconsistent with other soundly based rules, has been riddled with inconsistent exceptions, or is manifestly inequitable or unjust, and the value of overruling the rule exceeds the value of retaining it.

1   A BRIEF INTRODUCTION
TO THE COMMON LAW

One of two legal systems prevails in most developed economies: common law or civil law. The purpose of this book is to consider, explain, and analyze legal reasoning in the common law, and more particularly in American common law.

Law can be conceptualized as sets of binary categories. One set consists of public law and private law. Public law concerns such matters as the organization of government, the relations between the branches of government, other public matters, such as administrative, tax, and criminal law, and the relationships between government, on the one hand, and private individuals and institutions, on the other. Private law concerns such matters as the relationships between individuals, the relationships between individuals and private institutions, and the rights and obligations of individuals and private institutions.

A second set consists of common law and civil law systems.[1] In civil law systems public law is largely found in statutes and executive decrees, while private law is largely found in Civil Codes – codifications of the law concerning obligations, property, and family. In contrast, in common law systems, particularly American common law, public law

---

[1] Common law systems are in force in England, the United States, countries that like the United States began as English colonies, such as Australia, New Zealand and Canada (except Quebec), and other countries that had a connection with England. Civil law systems are in force in most or all European, South American, and Central American countries, and many or most Asian and sub-Saharan countries. In addition to civil law and common law, some developed economies have religious or mixed legal systems. Religious systems include Hindu law and Islamic or Sharia law. Mixed systems usually combine civil law and common law or civil law and religious law. *See* Vernon Valentine Parker, *Mixed Legal Systems—The Origin of the Species*, 28 TUL. EUR. & CIV. L. F. 103, 103–04 (2013).

is largely made by legislatures and administrative agencies, while private law is largely made by the courts, in the form of precedents, that is, judicial decisions. (There has been some convergence between common law and civil law systems, expressed principally in an increased significance of precedents in some civil law jurisdictions,[2] but there remains a fundamental difference between the two systems: In the common law a single precedent decided by an appellate court is law; in the civil law it is not.)

The reason why American private law is largely made by the courts is that complex societies need a great amount of private law to facilitate private planning, shape private conduct, and facilitate the settlement of private disputes, and the capacity of American legislatures to systematically make private law is limited.

To begin with, legislative time is limited and most of that time is devoted to public law.

Next, American legislatures are not staffed in a manner that enables them to comprehensively perform the function of making private law. So, for example, when an American legislature enacts a private-law statute frequently it does not draft the statute but instead adopts legislation proposed by nongovernmental organizations, such as the American Law Institute (ALI), the American Bar Association (ABA), or the Uniform Laws Commission. For example, the corporation law statutes of many states are based on the Model Business Corporation Act, which is drafted by a committee of the ABA. Other important statutes, including the Uniform Commercial Code, are taken from legislation proposed by the Uniform Laws Commission or jointly proposed by the Commission and the ALI.

Given the need to have a great deal of private law and the incapacity of American legislatures to systematically fill that need most

---

[2] Robert Alexy and Ralf Dreier report that precedents are cited in 95 percent or more cases in Germany's highest courts but add that "the jurisprudence [here meaning law] of the courts does not treat precedents as sources of law independent of statute and custom." Robert Alexy & Ralf Dreier, *Precedent in the Federal Republic of Germany, in* INTERPRETING PRECEDENTS: A COMPARATIVE STUDY 17, 23, 26–27, 32 (D. Neil MacCormick & Robert S. Summers eds., 1997). In France "the word 'precedent' never means a binding decision because courts are never bound by precedents." Michel Troper & Christophe Grezegorczyk, *Precedent in France, in* INTERPRETING PRECEDENTS, *supra*, 103, at 111. In some Civil Code jurisdictions precedents may play a significant role where the relevant Code does not provide a rule or provides only a very general rule, which the courts may then fill out with a line of precedents.

American private law is made by the courts. Accordingly, American common law courts have two functions: resolving disputes by the application of legal rules and making legal rules. *Cukor* v. *Mikalauskus*,[3] decided by the Pennsylvania Supreme Court, is a good example of judicial lawmaking. Corporate directors, officers, and controlling shareholders are unlikely to sue themselves for their own wrongdoing. The courts therefore developed the rule that shareholders have the power to bring derivative actions (actions brought by a shareholder on the corporation's behalf) against directors, officers, and controlling shareholders to remedy such wrongdoing. However, the courts also developed limits on that power. One limit is that subject to certain exceptions a shareholder who wants to bring a derivative action must first make a demand on the board to bring the action on the corporation's behalf. In *Cukor* a shareholder in PECO Energy Co. brought a derivative action against PECO directors and officers on the ground that they had engaged in wrongdoing, and PECO's board moved to terminate the action on the basis of a report by a special litigation committee that concluded that the action was not in the corporation's best interests. To resolve the case the Pennsylvania Supreme Court made a number of new rules of Pennsylvania law. The court said:

> The considerations and procedures applicable to derivative actions are all encompassed in Part VII, chapter 1 of the *ALI Principles [of Corporate Governance]* ..., which provides a comprehensive mechanism to address shareholder derivative actions. A number of its provisions are implicated in the action at bar. Sections 7.02 (standing), 7.03 (the demand rule), 7.04 (procedure in derivative action), 7.05 (board authority in derivative action), 7.06 (judicial stay of derivative action), 7.07, 7.08, and 7.09 (dismissal of derivative action), 7.10 (standard of judicial review), and 7.13 (judicial procedures) are specifically applicable to this case. These sections set forth guidance which is consistent with Pennsylvania law and precedent, which furthers the policies inherent in the business judgment rule, and which provides an appropriate degree of specificity to guide the trial court in controlling the proceedings in this litigation.

[3] 692 A.2d 1042 (Pa. 1997).

> We specifically adopt ... the specified sections of the *ALI*
> *Principles* [as the law of Pennsylvania] ....[4]

Cukor v. *Mikalauskus* is a single instance of judicial lawmaking. Of
vastly more importance, great areas of American private law, such as
contracts, torts, and property, are largely judicially made.

---

[4] *Id.* at 1048–49. For those readers who are not members of the legal profession (judges,
practicing lawyers, and legal academics), the ALI is an organization composed of approxi-
mately 4,000 elected members of the profession. Its objective is to promote the clarification
and simplification of the law and its better adaptation to social needs. The ALI seeks to
achieve that objective largely through adopting and publishing Restatements of various
branches of the law. The theory of the Restatements is that the ALI should feel obliged in its
deliberations to give weight to all the considerations that the courts, under a proper view of
the judicial function, deem it right to consider in theirs. The *Principles of Corporate
Governance* is for the most part a Restatement of the law in that area. It sets out the legal
rules applicable to the governance of corporations, including derivative actions.

2   RULE-BASED LEGAL REASONING

Common law courts have two functions: resolving disputes according to legal rules and making legal rules. A common law rule is a relatively specific legal norm, established by the courts, that requires actors to act or not act in a specified manner, enables or disables specified types of arrangements (such as contracts) or dispositions (such as wills), or specifies remedies for designated wrongs. Reasoning in the common law is almost entirely rule-based, that is, based on the application of legal rules to the facts of the case to be decided.

Hernandez v. *Hammond Homes, Ltd.*[1] is an example of rule-based reasoning. Hammond Homes was in the business of building homes. It hired Felix Brito, a roofing contractor, to install a roof on a home that it was building. Hernandez worked as a roofer for Brito. While working on the Hammond roof he descended a ladder. The ladder slipped, and Hernandez fell and was paralyzed. Hernandez sued Hammond on the grounds of premises liability and negligence. Hammond moved for summary judgment on the ground that it had no duty to Hernandez because he was an employee of an independent contractor and Hammond exercised no control over the roofing activities related to Hernandez's injury. The trial court granted summary judgment for Hammond. The Texas Court of Appeals affirmed, based on a series of rules established in binding precedents. Here is an

---

[1] 345 S.W.2d 150 (Ct. App. Tex. 2011).

excerpt from that opinion; brackets are inserted to mark out the
legal rules the court applied:

> [1] Generally, an employer of an independent contractor does not
> owe a duty to ensure that the independent contractor performs its
> work in a safe manner. *Gen. Elec. Co. v. Moritz*, 257 S.W.3d 211,
> 214 (Tex. 2008); *Redinger v. Living, Inc.*, 689 S.W.2d 415, 418
> (Tex. 1985). [2] However, "one who retains a right to control the
> contractor's work may be held liable for negligence in exercising
> that right." *Moritz*, 257 S.W.3d at 214; *see Redinger*, 689 S.W.2d
> at 418 (adopting Restatement (Second) of Torts § 414 (1965)).
> [3] For liability to attach, "[t]he employer's role must be more than
> a general right to order the work to start or stop, to inspect
> progress or receive reports." *Dow Chem. Co. v. Bright*, 89 S.
> W.3d 602, 606 (Tex. 2002) . . .. [4] For a duty to arise, the control
> must be over the manner in which the independent contractor
> performs its work. *Lee Lewis Constr., Inc. v. Harrison*, 70 S.W.3d
> 778, 783 (Tex. 2001). [5] The employer's duty "is commensurate
> with the general control it retains over the independent contrac-
> tor's work." *Id.* [6] Also, "[t]he supervisory control retained or
> exercised must relate to the activity that actually caused the
> injury." *Coastal Marine Serv. of Tex., Inc. v. Lawrence*, 988 S.
> W.2d 223, 226 (Tex. 1999) (per curiam). *See Moritz*, 257 S.
> W.3d at 215; *Hagins v. E–Z Mart Stores, Inc.*, 128 S.W.3d 383,
> 388–89 (Tex. App. – Texarkana 2004, no pet.). [7] A party can
> prove a right to control in two ways: first, by evidence of
> a contractual agreement that explicitly assigns the employer
> a right to control; and second, in the absence of a contractual
> agreement, by evidence that the employer actually exercised con-
> trol over the manner in which the independent contractor per-
> formed its work. *Dow Chem. Co.*, 89 S.W.3d at 606; *Coastal
> Marine Serv.*, 988 S.W.2d at 226. [8] If a written contract assigns
> the right to control to the employer, then the plaintiff need not
> prove an actual exercise of control to establish a duty. *See Pollard
> v. Mo. Pac. R.R. Co.*, 759 S.W.2d 670, 670 (Tex. 1988) (per
> curiam). [9] However, if the contract does not explicitly assign
> control over the manner of work to the employer, then the plaintiff
> must present evidence of the actual exercise of control by the
> employer. *See Dow Chem. Co.*, 89 S.W.3d at 606; *Hagins*, 128 S.
> W.3d at 388–89. In this case there was no written contract
> between [Hammond and Brito] . . . and the evidence does not

raise a genuine issue of material fact regarding [Hammond's] actual exercise of control over Brito's employees' performance of their work.

ANALOGY-BASED LEGAL REASONING

Some commentators claim that reasoning in the common law is analogy-based rather than rule-based. For example, Lloyd Weinreb claimed that "There is something distinctive about legal reasoning, which is its reliance on analogy."[2] Emily Sherwin claims that "According to traditional understanding judges engage in a special form of legal reasoning, the method of reasoning by analogy."[3] Scott Brewer claims that "[L]egal argument is often associated with 'reasoning ... by analogy; indeed if metaphor is the dreamwork of language then analogy is the brainstorm of jurists."[4] Cass Sunstein claims that "Much of legal reasoning is analogical .... Analogical reasoning is pervasive in law."[5] Gerald Postema claims that "The distinctive technique of the common law discipline is analogical thinking."[6]

These claims are incorrect; common law courts seldom reason by analogy. I base this on three sets of data, one positive, one negative, and one experimental.

The positive set of data consists of the several thousand common law cases I have read. Few of these cases reasoned by analogy.

The negative set of data consists of the paucity of case citations by commentators who claim that legal reasoning is reasoning by analogy. Only two of these commentators cited even a single case to support

[2] LLOYD WEINREB, LEGAL REASON: THE USE OF ANALOGY IN LEGAL ARGUMENT 4 (2d ed. 2016).
[3] Emily Sherwin, *A Defense of Analogical Reasoning in Law*, 66 U. CHI. L. REV. 1178, 1179–80 (1999).
[4] Scott Brewer, *Exemplary Reasoning: Semantics, Pragmatics, and the Rational Force of Argument by Analogy*, 109 HARV. L. REV. 925, 926 (1996).
[5] CASS SUNSTEIN, LEGAL REASONING AND POLITICAL CONFLICT 62–63 (1996).
[6] Gerald J. Postema, *Philosophy of the Common Law*, in THE OXFORD HANDBOOK OF JURISPRUDENCE AND PHILOSOPHY OF LAW 588, 603 (2012). *See also* STEVEN J. BURTON, AN INTRODUCTION TO LAW AND LEGAL THINKING 25–26 (1985) ("[T]he central tenet of the common law is the principle of stare decisis .... Reasoning under the principle of stare decisis is reasoning by example or by analogy."

their claim, and both cited the same. If these commenters had been able to cite a number of cases to support their claim they would have done so. They didn't because they couldn't, since very few common law cases reason by analogy.

The experimental set of data was derived as follows: First, I selected three Regional Reporters at random – 345 South Western 2d, 65 Southern 3d, and 713 South Eastern 2d.[7] I then reviewed all the common law cases in these three volumes – eighty-four in all. The result was as follows: only *three* of the eighty-four cases involved reasoning by analogy.[8]

The reason so few common law cases reason by analogy is simple: a court will never reason by analogy if the case before it is governed by a binding legal rule and the common law is rich with binding legal rules.

SIMILARITY-BASED LEGAL REASONING

Some commentators claim that legal reasoning depends on a finding of similarity between a precedent case and the case to be decided. For example, Fred Schauer claims that "in order to determine what is a precedent for what, we must engage in some determination of the relevant similarities between the two events"[9] and "[it must be determined] whether there is a relevant similarity between some possible precedent case and the instant case, for only when there is will the instant court be under an obligation to follow what the precedent court said."[10] Similarly, Cass Sunstein claims that judges "look for relevant similarities and relevant differences."[11]

---

[7] For readers who are not members of the legal profession, Regional Reporters publish all or most of the cases decided by state courts in a given region. For example, the South Western Reporter publishes cases decided by the courts in Arkansas, Kentucky, Missouri, Tennessee, and Texas. Any given volume of a Regional Reporter publishes all or most of the cases in its region that were decided during a given period of time. For example, volume 346 South Western 2d published most or all of those cases that were decided in July and August 1998.

[8] One who wishes to test or verify this experiment can do so by reviewing the Reporters I reviewed or any other Reporters to determine if they contained significantly more common law cases that reasoned by analogy than I found.

[9] Frederick Schauer, *Precedent*, 39 STAN. L. REV. 571, 577 (1987).

[10] FREDERICK SCHAUER, THINKING LIKE A LAWYER 45 (2009).

[11] SUNSTEIN, *supra* note 5, at 77.

These claims are also incorrect. Under the principle of stare decisis if a case is governed by a binding rule established in a precedent that was decided by a superior court or by the deciding court itself, the deciding court must apply that rule, subject to the limits of the principle. A deciding court would never reason by similarity if the case before it was governed by a binding legal rule.

With that background, suppose first that there is a binding prior case that is extremely similar to a case to be decided. Such a case would almost certainly have established a rule that governed its decision. Accordingly, the deciding court would almost certainly base its decision on that rule, not on similarity.

Suppose next that there is no extremely similar prior case, but there is a prior case that is loosely similar to the case to be decided. In that event, neither stare decisis nor any other principle of legal reasoning would require the deciding court to follow the prior case. Of course, the deciding court might follow the prior case just because it is loosely similar to the case before it, even though no principle of legal reasoning requires it to do so. However, that is very unlikely. If the case before the deciding court is not governed by a binding legal rule the court is much more likely to apply an authoritative although not binding rule (see Chapter 5), or to establish a new rule, because either course would involve much crisper reasoning than following a prior case because it is loosely similar to the case to be decided.

The proof of the pudding is in the eating. Of the several thousand cases I have read, few involved reasoning by similarity; neither Schauer nor Sunstein cite a single case in which a court reasoned by similarity; and in the experiment described earlier, in which I reviewed eighty-four common law cases selected at random, only one reasoned by similarity.

APPENDIX

Larry Alexander's Rule Model of Precedent

Larry Alexander has developed a model of common law reasoning that he calls the rule model of precedent.[12] Under this model "the precedent court has authority not only to decide the case before it but also to promulgate a general rule binding on courts of subordinate and equal

---

[12] Larry Alexander, *Constrained by Precedent*, 63 S. Cal. L. Rev. 1 (1989).

rank. The rule will operate as a statute and will, like a statute, have a canonical formulation."[13] Alexander's rule model is comparable to rule-based legal reasoning in some respects but differs in others.

To begin with, Alexander argued that

> one problem with the rule model of precedent is its requirement that cases contain discernible rules in order to operate as precedents. This is a problem because many cases clearly fail this condition. For instance, some cases lack discernible rules because the court's opinion is particularly opaque, cryptic, or self-contradictory. Other cases lack discernible rules because the majority of the court is divided into factions, each of which offers a different rule, and no rule commands a majority of the court.[14]

If it were correct that many precedents do not contain discernible rules, that would call into question the proposition that legal reasoning is rule-based. However, Alexander's characterization of common law precedents is incorrect. The rules established in American common law precedents are seldom, if ever, opaque, cryptic, self-contradictory, or expressed in opinions in which no rule commands a majority. On the contrary, almost all American common law precedents establish rules that are clear, not cryptic; straightforward, not opaque; internally consistent, not self-contradictory; and adopted either unanimously or by a majority of the judges.[15]

Here are four illustrative cases:

In *Louise Caroline Nursing Home, Inc.* v. *Dix Construction Co.*,[16] the issue was the measure of damages for a contractor's failure to complete a construction contract. The court held that the measure of damages in such a case is the reasonable cost of completing the contractor's defective performance less any part of the contract price that has not been paid.

[13] *Id.* at 17–18.
[14] *Id.* at 27. For a comparable position, *see* Michael Moore, *Precedent, Induction, and Ethical Generalization, in* PRECEDENT IN THE LAW 184–88 (Lawrence Goldstein ed., 1987).
[15] It is important to distinguish between whether a rule established in a precedent is clear and whether it is clear that a new case falls within the rule. For example, it is a well-established rule of contract law that if an offeree rejects an offer, its power of acceptance is terminated. That rule is clear, but whether an offeree's statement constitutes a rejection may sometimes not be clear.
[16] 362 Mass. 306 (1972).

Very clear – not opaque, cryptic, or self-contradictory, and not decided by a divided court.

In *Aiello Construction, Inc.* v. *Nationwide Tractor Trailer Training and Placement Co.*,[17] the issue was the measure of damages for breach by a person who contracted to have services performed. The court held that damages in such cases should be measured by the contractor's expenditures to the date of breach less the value of any materials still at hand plus the profits the contractor would have realized from full performance. Very clear – not opaque, cryptic, or self-contradictory, and not decided by a divided court.

In *Vitex Mfg. Corp.* v. *Caribtex Corp.*,[18] the issue was whether a buyer's overhead should be included in its costs for the purposes of determining its lost profit resulting from a seller's breach of a contract to deliver a commodity that the buyer intended to process and then sell. The court held that a seller's overhead should not be included in its costs in determining its lost profit. Very clear – not opaque, cryptic, or self-contradictory, and not decided by a divided court.

In *Valentine* v. *General American Credit, Inc.*,[19] the issue was whether an employee could recover damages for mental distress that resulted from the employee having been discharged in breach of her employment contract. The court held that an employee could not recover such damages. Very clear – not opaque, cryptic, or self-contradictory, and not decided by a divided court.

These are only four cases, but most common law cases have the same structure.

Problems may arise in dealing with common law rules, but lack of clarity is usually not one of them. Instead, the most common problems are whether the rule is applicable to the case, whether the rule is distinguishable from the case, whether an exception to the rule should be made, or whether the rule is unsound and should be overruled.

Alexander also argued that "Under the rule model, the [deciding] court faces a binary choice: It can either follow the precedent rule in its canonical form or overrule it. *All modifications of the rule . . . amount to*

---

[17] 22 R.I. 861 (1980).

[18] 377 F.2d 795 (3d Cir. 1967).

[19] 420 Mich. 256 (1984). I selected these four cases by skimming through LON L. FULLER, MELVIN A. EISENBERG & MARK GERGEN, BASIC CONTRACT LAW (10th ed. 2018).

overruling the precedent rule and replacing it with a new rule."[20] This too is incorrect. A common law rule can be modified without being directly or indirectly overruled. For example, specific new rules can be hived off from a general common law rule without overruling the general rule. Thus until the 1940s it was a general rule of contract law that donative promises are unenforceable. Then a new rule was hived off under which relied-upon donative promises *are* enforceable. The general rule was not overruled: rather, it continued to stand side-by-side with the specific hived-off rule.

Similarly, exceptions can be made to a common law rule without overruling it. For example, it was early established as a general rule of contract law that bargains are enforceable, but eventually a number of exceptions to the general rule were made. Thus unconscionable bargains are unenforceable and a bargain made by a minor is not enforceable against the minor. None of the exceptions overruled the general rule. The general rule continues to stand, subject to the exceptions.

Finally, and perhaps most important, common law rules are not canonical, as statutes are. On the contrary, they are malleable. See Chapter 8.

---

[20] *Id.* at 19 (emphasis in original).

3 REASONING FROM PRECEDENT AND THE PRINCIPLE OF STARE DECISIS

The foundation of rule-based reasoning is the principle of stare decisis, which is short for the Latin term stare decisis et non quieta movere, meaning to stand by things decided and not disturb settled matters. For purposes of legal reasoning, the important part of this term consists of the phrase to stand by things decided. Under the principle of stare decisis when a court decides a case that is governed by a rule established in a precedent decided by a superior court or by the deciding court itself the court must apply that rule, subject to the limits of the principle. As Larry Alexander and Emily Sherwin write, under the principle of stare decisis "courts should apply previously announced rules to present cases that fall within the rules' terms even when the courts' own best judgment, all things considered, points to a different result."[1]

Reasoning from precedent and the principle of stare decisis raise a series of questions. What is a precedent? What is the justification of the principle of stare decisis? What are the limits on the principle of stare decisis? How is it determined what rule a precedent establishes? These and other questions are addressed in this chapter and Chapter 4.

WHAT IS A PRECEDENT?

In everyday speech the term *precedent* has two meanings. One meaning is descriptive. For example, in everyday speech the term may refer to

---

[1] Larry Alexander and Emily Sherwin, *Judges as Rule Makers, in* COMMON LAW THEORY 1 (Dougas Edlin ed., 2007).

past conduct that shows that a certain type of conduct is not unusual, as in "There is precedent for running meetings this way," or is practicable, as in "There is precedent for mining sapphires this way."

The second meaning of precedent in everyday speech is normative. This meaning applies where the term refers to an act or a course of conduct that one or more persons can reasonably expect the actor to repeat if similar circumstances arise in the future, as the actor knows or should know. Typically, a precedent of this type is invoked against the actor by a person who claims a moral right to require the actor follow the precedent. Such a claim may be based on the ground that the precedent gave rise to a reasonable expectation that it would be followed by the actor in the future, as in "You have always given your employees a one hour lunch break and this gave us, your employees, reason to expect that you would continue that practice." Or such a claim may be based on a demand for equal treatment, as in "You let my sister begin to drive when she was sixteen and you should let me begin to drive at that age too." Because acts may constitute normative precedents it is not uncommon for an actor to preclude a future claim by stating, "This act will not set a precedent." Alternatively, an actor may decide not to engage in an act out of concern that doing so would give rise to a future claim based on precedent.

In law the term precedent also has two meanings. It can simply mean a decided case. For example, in his book review *Comparing Precedent*[2] John Bell states that "a large number of judicial decisions [in civil law jurisdictions] ... make reference to precedent"[3] and "we know that the judges [in civil law jurisdictions] did actually read the precedents and discuss them in private sessions although they did not cite them in their opinions."[4] Since a single case is not law in civil law jurisdictions Bell here uses the term *precedent* to mean a decided case. In American law, however, the term precedent usually means a decided case that is binding on subordinate courts and the same court. (That is the meaning employed in this book, and for ease of exposition the terms *precedent* and *binding precedent* are used interchangeably.)

[2] John Bell, *Comparing Precedent*, 82 CORNELL L. REV. 1243 (1997).
[3] *Id.* at 1248.
[4] *Id.* at 1249.

Here lies the difference between the meaning of precedent in everyday speech and its legal meaning. In everyday speech an actor may be morally bound to follow a normative precedent but not legally bound to do so. In law a subordinate court and the same court must apply the rule established in a binding precedent unless the court overrules the rule, hives off a new rule, makes an exception to the rule, or distinguishes the rule. (Hiving off, making exceptions, and drawing distinctions are discussed in Chapter 9 and overruling is discussed in Chapter 13.)

THE JUSTIFICATION OF THE PRINCIPLE OF STARE DECISIS

As the great judge Benjamin Cardozo said the principle of stare decisis "is the everyday working rule of our law."[5] The principle is supported by all American courts and all but a few commentators. However, notwithstanding this virtually unanimous support for the principle, the justification of the principle is contested.

One proffered justification is based on efficiency. "[T]he labor of judges," Cardozo added, "would be increased to the breaking point if every past decision could be reopened in every case."[6] Or as Judge Harris Hartz of the Tenth Federal Circuit commented on an earlier draft of this chapter:

> I remember the joy I experienced as a judge when I realized that I did not have to resolve every issue from scratch .... It is unusual for an opinion of mine to include more than a few sentences that say something original about the law. I don't have to think about the standard of review for fact finding by the trial jury or judge, who has the burden of persuasion on an issue, etc.

Nevertheless, the power of this justification is limited, because in most cases involving stare decisis the issue is not whether to reopen a decided case but whether a decided case *is* a precedent for a case to be decided, what rule a precedent established, and how that rule applies to

---

[5] BENJAMIN J. CARDOZO, THE NATURE OF THE JUDICIAL PROCESS 20 (1921). Accord: *Hubbard* v. *United States* 514 U.S. 695 (1994) (opinion of Stevens, J.).

[6] CARDOZO, *supra* note 5, at 149.

the case before the court. Furthermore, given the importance of the principle of stare decisis most commentators have sought a justification of the principle that carries greater moral and policy weight than efficiency. As Judge Hartz continued, "Persons who are not judges would have little interest in supporting the doctrine [of stare decisis] if efficiency were the only justification. Prosecutors and defense attorneys justify plea bargaining on efficiency grounds, but it is rare to hear someone who is not in the business praising the practice."

Another proffered justification of the principle of stare decisis is that under the principle judges know that their decisions will affect future cases and therefore must look beyond the cases before them to the effect of their decisions in the future. To put this differently, under the principle of stare decisis a judge is forced to lay down rules to govern not only the present case but cases in the proximate future. But the force of this justification is also limited because most judges probably would take the future impact of their decisions into account even without the principle of stare decisis.

Still another proffered justification of the principle of stare decisis is based on the proposition that fairness requires like cases to be treated alike, and therefore it would be unfair to treat a case that is to be decided differently from a like decided case. So, for example, Bryan Garner begins the book *The Law of Judicial Precedent* with the rule that "Like cases should be treated alike."[7] There is certainly value in treating like cases alike, but that value does not explain the principle of stare decisis either descriptively or normatively.

Descriptively, a huge number of like cases are treated differently rather than the same because the principle of stare decisis is subject to important limits. For example, the principle does not require a case decided in State A to be treated the same as a like case decided in State B. Nor does it require a case decided by one federal Circuit of Appeals to be decided the same as a like case decided in another Circuit. So too stare decisis usually does not require a case decided by a state intermediate court of appeals to be treated the same as a like case decided by

---

[7] BRYAN A. GARNER ET AL., THE LAW OF JUDICIAL PRECEDENT 21 (2016). This book has thirteen authors. I attribute the quote to Garner since he drafted the black letter of each section.

a sister intermediate court.[8] And stare decisis does not require a case to be decided by a trial court the same way as like cases decided by other trial courts in the same jurisdiction.

The argument that stare decisis is justified by the principle that like cases should be treated alike is also subject to important normative criticisms. For one thing, no two cases are conclusively alike. As David Lyon writes:

> I shall call the idea that the practice of precedent respects the requirement that like cases be treated alike, *the formal justice argument*. . . .
>
> One aspect of the formal justice argument needs to be considered first: both the premise and the conclusion incorporate the problematic notion of a "like" or "similar" case. . . .
>
> The basic problem is simple. Take any case that is to be decided and any other case that has already been decided. However similar they may be, in respects that may seem important, they will also be different in some respects, and vice versa. Some general facts about one case will be general facts about the other, and some general facts about one case will not be general facts about the other. So objective grounds exist both for *and* against regarding *any* past case as "similar" to one that is to be decided.
>
> As a consequence, a principle prescribing that decisions follow those that have already been made in "similar cases" can seem literally impossible to follow. If all the factual aspects of cases were relevant, and any similarity and any difference between cases were sufficient to make them similar and different, respectively, then each past case would both be and not be a precedent for any case to be decided. On that interpretation, the principle would be impossible to follow because it would be, strictly speaking, incoherent.[9]

Next, if the principle of treating like cases alike is based on justice it lacks force when the application of the rule established in the precedent would not comport with morality. This point is very well made by Larry Alexander:

> Suppose that when my daughter reaches the age of thirteen, she requests permission from me to attend a rock concert. I weigh the possible risks involved in her going and the potential benefits to our

[8] *See, e.g., Mountain View Coach v. Storms*, 102 A.D.2d 663 (App. Div. 1984).

[9] David Lyons, *Formal Justice and Judicial Precedent*, 38 VAND. L. REV. 495, 498–99 (1985) (emphasis in original).

relationship, and I decide to grant her permission to go. When my son reaches the age of thirteen and also seeks permission to attend a rock concert, he predictably will cite my previous decision granting permission to his sister as a reason for a decision in his favor. . . .

If I tell my son that I will not permit him to attend the rock concert and that I should not have permitted his sister to go, he predictably will claim that I have not treated him equally with respect to her. By saying so . . . he will be making the normative claim that [the] dissimilarity in treatment is wrong in the absence of countervailing considerations of substantial moral weight. In other words, he will be asserting that the value of equality is a sufficiently weighty reason in support of letting him go to the concert that it tips the balance of reasons in his favor. . . .

[But] if the dangers of allowing a thirteen-year-old to attend the concert outweigh the pleasures, and if my responsibility as a parent is such that I should not allow my children to attend under those circumstances, then my mistake regarding my daughter should carry no weight in deciding whether to grant my son's request. It would be a perversion of the role of equality as a moral value to invoke it as a reason to endanger my son's welfare. My response to my son's predictable complaint of unequal treatment is that it is his sister who has the true grievance, namely, that I endangered her by permitting her to attend. In sum, the sense of equality that carries moral weight cannot require perpetuation of otherwise immoral conduct.[10]

And again David Lyons:

[W]e are free to change our moral opinions honestly. The constraint of consistency does not mean that we are prohibited from modifying, qualifying, refining, or otherwise revising our moral judgments, including the standards we apply. We are free to reject judgments that we made in the past, if they can no longer be supported by standards we now accept . . . .[11]

Theodore Benditt made a related criticism of the treating-like-cases-alike justification of stare decisis:

[The] principle of justice (like cases are to be treated alike) implies only that if two relevantly similar cases are treated differently . . . then

[10] Larry Alexander, *Constrained by Precedent*, 63 S. CAL. L. REV. 1, 5–7, 10 (1989).
[11] Lyons, *supra* note 9, at 508.

some party has been treated unfairly, [but] the principle doesn't say which.[12]

That is, if a later case is treated differently than a like earlier case, the principle of treating like cases alike doesn't tell us whether a party to the later case or a party to the earlier case was treated unfairly. Therefore, treating like cases alike could simply require that the earlier case be upended if that is possible, not that the later case should be decided the same way. To put it differently, the question is, should a party to a later case have a right to complain about being treated differently than a party to a case that was decided years ago, which the later party didn't even know about when engaging in the relevant conduct? Or should a party to an earlier case, who is well out of the picture, have a right to complain about being treated differently from a party to the later case? Recall Alexander's hypothetical in which he does not allow his thirteen-year-old son to attend a rock concert despite the fact that he had previously allowed his then-thirteen-year-old daughter to do so: "My response to my son's predictable complaint of unequal treatment is that it is his sister who has the true grievance, namely, that I endangered her by allowing her to attend."

A better justification of stare decisis is that it provides stability to the common law. Stability of law should be and is given weight because it affords predictability of the law, and predictability of the law has social value. Stability of the law is achieved under the principle of stare decisis because under that principle courts should follow a rule established in a binding precedent even if it is not the best possible rule as long as it is substantially congruent with social morality, social policy, and experience, and therefore is a reasonably good rule. Small differences between the best possible rule and a reasonably good rule are likely to be debatable, difficult to perceive, or both. Therefore, if the courts failed to follow rules established in binding precedents just because they were modestly less desirable than competing rules it would be difficult if not impossible to rely on rules established in binding precedents. To put this

---

[12] Theodore M. Benditt, *The Rule of Precedent*, in PRECEDENT IN LAW 89, 90 (L. Goldstein ed., 1987).

differently, at least over the short term the value of making minor improvements in rules established in binding precedents is normally outweighed by the value of stability in the law. This stability is the product of the principle of stare decisis.

Finally I come to the best justification of the principle of stare decisis. Frank Easterbrook argues that "we do not have—never can have—a comprehensive theory of precedent."[13] The first part of Easterbrook's argument is correct: we do not have a comprehensive theory of precedent. The second part of his argument is incorrect: we can have such a theory. It is as follows: Complex societies need a great amount of private law to facilitate private planning, shape private conduct, and facilitate the settlement of private disputes. Because legislatures in the United States do not have the capacity or the ability to enact more than a limited number of private law rules the task of adopting private law largely falls to the courts. Without the principle of stare decisis, however, courts could not make law. Accordingly, the best justification of that principle is that in the absence of stare decisis cases would be only persuasive, not binding, so we wouldn't have tort law, we wouldn't have contract law, we wouldn't have property law – in fact, we wouldn't have the common law.[14] (Of course, we would still have law made by legislatures, but as discussed above the capacity of American legislatures to make private law on a systematic basis is limited.)

ARGUMENTS AGAINST THE PRINCIPLE OF STARE DECISIS

A few commentators have argued that the principle of stare decisis is undesirable because it requires courts to follow precedents that are wrong. For example, Peter Wesley-Smith argues that "Stare decisis cannot be law . . . [because] judges owe . . . fidelity, not to the pronouncements of

[13] Frank H. Easterbrook, *Stability and Reliability in Judicial Decisions*, 73 CORNELL L. REV. 422, 423 (1988).
[14] *See also* Jeremy Waldron, *Stare Decisis and the Rule of Law: A Layered Approach*, 111 MICH. L. REV. 1 (2012), which argues that the rule of law justifies the principle of *stare decisis*. I view this argument as supplementing rather than conflicting with the analysis in this chapter.

predecessors, but to the law."[15] Such arguments are not well-founded.

To begin with, stare decisis not only can be but *is* the law. Next, arguments against stare decisis tacitly assume that many precedents are seriously wrong – it would hardly be worth throwing over a basic principle of legal reasoning because a few precedents are seriously wrong. However, it is highly unlikely that many precedents are seriously wrong, partly because most appellate judges are competent, partly because most appellate judges sit on multijudge courts so that one incompetent judge is unlikely to carry the day, and partly because seriously wrong precedents are likely to fall within one of the limits on stare decisis discussed below. Among these limits is that if a rule adopted in a precedent is not even substantially congruent with social morality and social policy, a court may overrule or revise it.

In short, there is a cost to the principle of stare decisis because a few seriously wrong precedents may become law at least for a time. However, this cost is relatively low because very few legal rules are likely to be seriously wrong, and the benefit of the principle is great because as a result of that principle we have the common law.

VERTICAL AND HORIZONTAL STARE DECISIS

The principle of stare decisis exists in two dimensions – horizontal and vertical. Horizontal stare decisis requires courts to follow their own precedents. Vertical stare decisis requires subordinate courts to follow precedents decided by superior courts. Vertical stare decisis has more force than horizontal stare decisis. Under appropriate circumstances a superior court can overrule or revise a rule it previously established. In contrast, a subordinate court cannot overrule or revise a precedent decided by a superior court. Furthermore a superior court can escape the principle of stare decisis by invoking one of the limits on that principle, but that course is usually not open to a subordinate court

---

[15] Peter Wesley-Smith, *Theories of Adjudication and the Status of Stare Decisis, in* PRECEDENT IN LAW 73 (L. Goldstein ed., 1988). *See also* Christopher J. Peters, *Foolish Consistency: On Equality, Integrity, and Justice in Stare Decisis*, 105 YALE L. J. 1 (1996).

dealing with a precedent decided by a superior court. However, although horizontal stare decisis is not *as* strong as vertical stare decisis it *is* strong because it requires a court to follow rules established in its own precedents, subject to the limits on the principle.

THE LAW-OF-THE-CIRCUIT DOCTRINE

An important example of horizontal stare decisis is the law-of-the-Circuit doctrine. Decisions of federal Circuit Courts are normally rendered by three-judge panels rather than by the entire Circuit bench. Under the law-of-the-Circuit doctrine a decision by a panel is normally binding on future decisions by all panels in the Circuit. Some Circuits have adopted special rules limiting the stare decisis effect of panel decisions, but only under fairly rigorous conditions. In the First Circuit a panel decision need not be followed "in extremely rare circumstances, where non-controlling but persuasive case law suggests such a course"[16] or if a later panel circulates a proposed overruling decision to all the Circuit judges for comment and a majority of the judges do not object.[17] The Second and D.C. Circuits have similar procedures, except that in the Second Circuit it appears that a single judge might be able to prevent the overruling by objecting.[18] The Seventh Circuit has gone further by codifying the power of panels to overrule decisions of earlier panels.[19] The Tenth Circuit occasionally uses what it calls an en banc footnote. Under this procedure if a panel believes that a Circuit precedent is no longer tenable it will request authority from all the active judges to overturn the precedent. The request will be granted only if all the active judges agree.

---

[16] *United States* v. *Lewko*, 169 F.3d 64, 66 (1st Cir. 2001).
[17] *United States* v. *Dowdell*, 595 F.3d 60, 62 n.8 (1st Cir. 2010).
[18] GARNER ET AL., *supra* note 7, at 493.
[19] *See* Seventh Circuit Rule 40(e):

> Rehearing Sua Sponte Before Decision. A proposed opinion approved by a panel of this court adopting a position which would overrule a prior decision of this court or create a conflict between or among circuits shall not be published unless it is first circulated among the active numbers of this court and a majority of them do not vote to rehear en banc the issue of whether the position should be adopted.

JURISDICTIONAL AND SUBSTANTIVE LIMITS
ON THE PRINCIPLE OF STARE DECISIS

Jurisdictional Limits

Not every decided case is binding on every court. To understand what decisions are binding on what courts it is necessary to briefly describe the two judicial systems in the United States, federal and state.

At the top of the federal judicial system is the United States Supreme Court. At the bottom are trial courts, known as district courts. Between the Supreme Court and the district courts are thirteen intermediate Courts of Appeal, known as Circuit Courts of Appeal.[20] The decisions of the Supreme Court bind that Court and all subordinate courts. Decisions of district courts have no stare decisis effect: as stated by the Supreme Court in *Camreta* v. *Greene*[21] "a decision of a federal district court judge is not binding precedent in either a different judicial district, the same judicial district, or even upon the same judge in a different case." Circuit Court of Appeal en banc and panel decisions are binding on the Circuit Court sitting en banc and on panels in the same Circuit,[22] but neither en banc nor panel decisions are binding on other Circuit Courts.

The structure of state judicial systems parallels the structure of the federal system. The states too have a supreme court, trial courts, and intermediate appellate courts. Each intermediate appellate court has jurisdiction over appeals from trial courts in a designated area of the state. Decisions of a state supreme court bind that court and all

---

[20] The Circuit Courts of Appeal generally have jurisdiction over appeals from district courts sitting in a geographical area consisting of three to ten states or territories or, in the case of the D.C. Circuit, the District of Columbia. In addition to jurisdiction over appeals from district courts in the District of Columbia, the D.C. Circuit has exclusive appellate jurisdiction over appeals from certain federal administrative agencies. Plaintiffs who appeal decisions of other federal agencies are allowed to file their appeal either in the Circuit in which they reside or in the D.C. Circuit. *See Why Is the D.C. Circuit "So" Important*, CRS Reports and Analysis, May 31, 2013; Eric M. Fraser et al; *The Jurisdiction of the D.C. Circuit*, 23 CORNELL L. J. 1 (2013). The thirteenth Circuit Court, the Federal Circuit, has exclusive jurisdiction over certain subject areas, in particular patent cases.

[21] 563 U.S. 692, 709 n.7 (2011).

[22] *See, e.g., Sisney* v. *Reich*, 674 F.2d 839, 843 (8th Cir. 2012), *cert. denied*, 133 S. Ct. 359 (2012); *Brock* v. *Astrue*, 674 F.2d 1062 (8th Cir. 2012); In re Lambrix, 776 F.2d 789, 794 (11th Cir. 2015).

subordinate courts.[23] Decisions of trial courts have no stare decisis effect. The stare decisis effect of decisions by intermediate state courts varies. For example, in New York decisions of the intermediate appellate courts, known as the Supreme Courts, Appellate Division, do not bind other Appellate Divisions, but there is a split of authority on whether trial courts within the jurisdiction of one Appellate Division are bound by the decisions of other Appellate Divisions, although the majority view is that they are bound.[24]

Substantive Limits

There are a number of substantive limits on the principle of stare decisis. The most important limit is that in most areas of the common law if a rule established in a precedent is not even substantially congruent with social morality and social policy a court may overrule or revise the rule. The principle of stare decisis also tends to be inapplicable if the premise of the precedent was clearly erroneous, the rule established by the precedent has turned out to be unworkable, subsequent legal developments have unmoored the rule from its doctrinal anchor, subsequent factual developments have unmoored the rule from its factual anchor, or subsequent developments in social morality or social policy have unmoored the rule from its social anchor.

---

[23] *See, e.g., Mountain View Coach Lines* v. *Better Storms,* 102 A.D.2d 663 (1984); *United States* v. *Cooper,* 462 F.2d 1343 (1972).

[24] See Robert S. Summers, *Precedent in the United States (New York State), in* INTERPRETING PRECEDENTS (D. Neil McCormick & Robert S. Summers eds., 1997).

4 HOW IT IS DETERMINED WHAT RULE A PRECEDENT ESTABLISHES

The common law largely consists of rules established in precedents. This raises the question, how is it determined what rule a precedent establishes? The answer is that the rule established by a precedent is the rule that the precedent court stated governed the case before it.

In his article *Determining the Ratio Decidendi of a Case*,[1] Arthur Goodhart proposed a different theory: that a precedent stands for a rule consisting of the result of the precedent together with the facts that the precedent court deemed material. This theory is unsupportable.

First, courts seldom if ever single out some facts as material and there is no metric for objectively determining which facts a court deemed material.

Second, as Julius Stone demonstrated in his article *The Ratio of the Ratio Decidendi*[2] even if it could be determined what facts the precedent court deemed material every such fact could be stated at various levels of generality and each level would yield a different result.

Stone exemplified his critique with a famous British case, *Donoghue v. Stevenson*.[3] Donoghue's friend had purchased a bottle of ginger beer for her in a café. The bottle was opaque, and after Donoghue drank part of the ginger beer she discovered a decomposed snail in the bottle which could not have been detected until most of the ginger beer had been consumed. Donoghue suffered severe shock and gastroenteritis, sued the manufacturer, and won.

---

[1] Arthur Goodhart, *Determining the Ratio Decidendi of a Case*, 40 YALE L. J. 161 (1930).
[2] Julius Stone, *The Ratio of the Ratio Decidendi*, 22 MOD. L. REV. 507 (1959).
[3] [1932] L.R. App. Cas.562 (H.L. 1932).

Prior to *Donoghue* under English law the manufacturer of a defective product was ordinarily liable only to its immediate buyer – here, the café. It is clear that *Donoghue* rejected that rule, because the court held that the manufacturer was liable to Donoghue even though she was not the manufacturer's immediate buyer. However, Stone pointed out, under Goodhart's theory it would be far from clear just what rule the court adopted. Assume that the most important facts in *Donoghue* were those concerning the instrument of harm, the nature of the defendant, and the nature of Donoghue's injury. As Stone demonstrated, the instrument of harm could be described as a beverage, an opaque bottle of beverage, an opaque bottle of ginger beer, a chattel, or a container of liquids for consumption. The defendant could be characterized as a manufacturer, a manufacturer of nationally distributed goods, an entity working on goods, or an entity working on goods for profit. The injury could be characterized as an injury, a personal injury, a physical injury, or an emotional injury. Under Goodhart's theory, therefore, *Donoghue* could stand for a number of different rules. For example, it could stand for the rule that if a manufacturer of nationally distributed goods intended for consumption produced the goods negligently it is liable for any resulting injury. Or it could stand for the rule that if an entity working on goods for profit negligently produced defective goods it is liable for any resulting physical personal injury if it packaged the goods in such a way that the defect was concealed.

In short, a precedent does not stand for a rule consisting of its result together with the facts the precedent court deemed material. Rather, a precedent stands for the rule established in its holding, that is, the rule the precedent court stated determined the result in the case. This principle is forcefully supported by a masterful article by Peter Tiersma, *The Textualization of Precedent*.[4] Tiersma showed that, whatever might have been the case fifty years ago, today the holdings of common-law courts resemble statutes:

> It should be evident by now that . . . in determining the holding . . . of a case, there is substantial emphasis on the court's exact words. Half a century ago there were still prominent American legal

---

[4] Peter Tiersma, *The Textualization of Precedent*, 82 NOTRE DAME L. REV. 1187 (2007), © Notre Dame Law Review.

scholars, like Roscoe Pound, who could insist that the language of judicial opinions was not authoritative, but that it is the result that counts. Likewise, Edward Levi's influential book on legal reasoning stated that where case law is concerned, the judge "is not bound by the statement of the rule of law made by the prior judge even in the controlling case." Henry Hart and Albert Sacks could still seriously maintain, in their influential teaching materials on the legal process, that the ratio decidendi of a case "is not imprisoned in any single set of words" and that it therefore "has a flexibility which the statute does not have." Yet even as these scholars were writing, the ground beneath them was starting to shift. The language of judicial opinions was, and still is, becoming ever more textual.

What was once aptly described as a "case law" regime is well on its way to becoming an "opinion law" system. In other words, the precedential value of a case is nowadays determined not so much by analysis of the facts, the issue, and the outcome, but by careful scrutiny of the words written in the opinion. Especially noteworthy is that American courts are beginning to state their holdings explicitly, and that those statements of the holding are being treated more and more like a statute. Judicial opinions – or at least, the part that we regard as precedent or the holding – are gradually being textualized. . . .

More than two decades ago, Guido Calabresi wrote [that statutes often became obsolete]. . . . Calabresi's proposed remedy was to allow courts to update antiquated statutes. In essence, courts would treat legislation as though it were part of the common law. But what Calabresi anticipated has not come to pass. Rather than treating statutes as common law, courts are beginning to treat the common law as legislation.

A NOTE ON HOLDINGS, DICTA, RATIO DECIDENDI, AND JUSTIFICATIONS

Holdings

A holding is the rule that a court states determines the case before it. Accordingly, the terms *holding* and *the rule that a precedent establishes* are synonymous. The holding of a case is almost invariably easy to determine, and holdings are binding legal rules.

Take, for example, the famous case of *Hadley* v. *Baxendale*.[5] Hadley
was co-owner of a mill that had gone down because the crankshaft that
operated the mill had fractured. The crankshaft was manufactured by
Joyce & Co., at Greenwich, and Hadley wanted to ship the broken
crankshaft to Joyce to serve as a pattern for a new one. Pickford & Co.,
whose managing director was Baxendale, agreed to ship the crankshaft
to Joyce in one day, through London,[6] but then to save costs it made
other shipping arrangements, which delayed the delivery of the new
crankshaft.[7] As a result, Hadley received the new crankshaft several
days late and lost the profits he would have made if the delivery to Joyce
had been made as promised. Hadley sued Baxendale for his lost profits.

The issue in the case was, what must be the connection between
a promisor's breach of contract and the loss to the promisee. To resolve
this issue the court adopted what became known as the first and second
rules of *Hadley* v. *Baxendale:* "[The innocent party's damages for]
breach of contract should be [1] such as may fairly and reasonably be
considered either arising naturally, i.e., according to the usual course of
things, from such breach of contract itself, or [2] such as may reasonably be supposed to have been in the contemplation of both parties, at
the time they made the contract, as the probable result of the breach of
it." That is the holding of the case. Very clear.

Or take *Angel* v. *Murray*, decided by the Rhode Island Supreme
Court.[8] Often, parties to a contract enter into a modification of the
contract under which one of them, A, promises to pay the other, B,
more than B was entitled to, in exchange for B's promise to perform the
contract. Under a rule of classical contract law known as the preexisting
duty rule A's promise was unenforceable. This rule is unsound,
because a modification is a bargain and bargains should normally be
enforceable. In *Angel* v. *Murray* the Rhode Island Supreme Court

---

[5] 9 Exch. 341 (1854).

[6] *See* Richard Danzig, *Hadley* v. *Baxendale: A Study in the Industrialization of the Law*, 4
J. LEGAL STUD. 249 (1975).

[7] Instead of forwarding the crankshaft immediately by wagon from London to Greenwich,
Pickford kept the crankshaft in London for several days and then forwarded it to Greenwich
by barge, rather than wagon, along with tons of iron goods that had been consigned to
Joyce. RICHARD DANZIG & GEOFFREY R. WATSON, THE CAPABILITY PROBLEM IN CONTRACT
LAW (2d ed. 2004).

[8] 322 A. 630 (R.I. 1974).

adopted a new rule to take its place. Under this rule a promise modifying a duty under a contract that is not fully performed on either side is binding if the modification is fair and equitable in view of circumstances not anticipated by the parties when the contract was made, or to the extent that justice requires enforcement in view of a material change of position in reliance on the promise. That is the holding of the case. Very clear.

Hadley v. *Baxendale* and *Angel* v. *Murray* are exemplary, not unique. In almost all common law cases the court states the rule that determines the case. This rule is the holding, and holdings are almost invariably clear. Of course, holdings may require interpretation, but that does not mean that holdings are not rules, any more than the fact that statutes often require interpretation means that statutes are not rules.

Dicta

Most statements in judicial opinions fall into one of two categories: factual and legal. Factual statements consist of the facts and history of the case. The central legal statement is the holding of the case. Most other legal statements in a case are dicta – singular, dictum. Dictum is a Latin word meaning "something said," short for "obiter dictum," meaning something said in passing. Dicta concern rules but are not rules. Typically, dicta signal a court's possible future actions. For example, a dictum may be a a criticism of an established rule that does not rise to the level of undoing the rule.

Unlike holdings, dicta are not binding. The line between a holding and a dictum in a given case is usually – but not always – clear, and sometimes the line is manipulated by a court that does not want to follow a precedent but does not want to formally overrule it either, and avoids following the precedent by claiming, often disingenuously, that the holding of the precedent was really dictum because it went further than the facts of the case or was unnecessary for the decision.

Because dicta are not binding a common view is that dicta have no legal import. That view is greatly exaggerated. For example, Shawn Bayern in his article *Case Interpretation*[9] shows that as stated in *Doughy*

---

[9] Shawn Bayern, *Case Interpretation*, 36 Fla. State U. L. J. 125 (2000).

v. *Underwriters at Lloyds, London*,[10] "carefully considered language of the Supreme Court, even if technically dictum, generally must be treated as authoritative." Or, as stated in *Reich* v. *Continental Cas. Co.*[11] "[where language in] a recent Supreme Court dictum ... considers all the relevant considerations and adumbrates an unmistakable conclusion, it would be reckless to think that the Court is likely to adopt a contrary view in the near future." In short, as stated by Judge Pierre Leval: "[D]icta often serve extremely valuable purposes. ... They can assist future courts to reach sensible, well-reasoned results. They can help lawyers and society to predict the future course of the court's ruling. They can guide future courts to adopt fair and efficient procedures."[12]

Finally, dicta may be employed to foreshadow changes in the law and thereby put the profession on notice that an established rule may no longer be reliable.

Ratio Decidendi

Ratio decidendi is a Latin term that means the reason for or rationale of a decision. The term is used only occasionally in American common law cases because in American cases the holding, not the rationale of the holding, is binding, and the holding is almost invariably clear. In contrast, the term ratio decidendi is frequently used in English cases. Here is why. Both American and English appellate courts consist of three or more judges. In most American common law cases either all or a majority of the judges concur in the holding and most American common law cases have a clear holding. In contrast, in cases decided by English appellate courts it is not unusual for the judges to render separate opinions, so there is no clear holding. For example, in *Koufos* v. *Czarnikow, Ltd.*[13] the judges rendered five different opinions. In such cases the rule that a precedent stands for must be constructed from the separate opinions. This constructed rule is the ratio decidendi

---

[10] 6 F.3d 856, 861 (1st Cir. 1993).
[11] 33 F.3d 754, 757 (7th Cir. 1994).
[12] Pierre N. Leval, *Judging Under the Constitution, Dicta About Dicta*, 81 N.Y.U. L. Rev. 1249, 1253 (2006).
[13] [1969] 3 A.C. 350 (H.L. 1967).

of the case.[14] Thus, the concept of a ratio decidendi, which refers to a constructed rule, has little to do with the concept of a holding, which is an explicit rule.

Justifications

All common-law rules must ultimately be justified by propositions of social morality, social policy, and experience. Justifications differ from holdings and dicta. Holdings are rules. Justifications are not rules. Neither are justifications dicta. Dicta normally relate to the future. Justifications relate to the past or the present.

Because a justification is not a rule a court cannot decide a case by applying a justification. However, a court may employ a justification to make a new rule, which it then applies. Also, a court may employ the justification of a rule to determine how the rule should be interpreted and applied.

Frederick Schauer argues that "The common law appears ... to be decision according to justification rather than decision according to rule."[15] This argument is incorrect; if the common law consisted of justifications rather than rules it would be difficult if not impossible to determine what the common law is because a precedent can usually be justified in several ways. As Larry Alexander said, "there is an indefinite number of possible ... sets of principles that can 'justify' the results in ... precedent cases."[16] Furthermore, different justifications will often point in different directions.

Moreover, contrary to the premise of Schauer's argument even the most casual review will show that common-law courts seldom provide a justification of rules they apply. When a court states the rule that if an offeree rejects an offer the offeree's power of acceptance is terminated it will cite a precedent that establishes the rule, but seldom if ever add the justification of the rule. When a court states that a relied-upon donative promise is enforceable it will cite section 90 of Restatement of Contracts but seldom if ever add the justification of section 90.

---

[14] *See* Grant Lamond, *Precedent and Analogy in Legal Reasoning, in* STANFORD ENCYCLOPEDIA OF PHILOSOPHY 6 (2019).

[15] *Id.* at 178.

[16] Larry Alexander, *Constrained by Precedent*, 63 S. CAL. L. REV. 1, 38 (1989).

THE VIEW OF SOME, PERHAPS MOST, U.S. CIRCUIT COURT OF APPEAL PANELS ON WHAT CONSTITUTES A HOLDING AND ON STARE DECISIS

The definition of a holding and the operation of the principle of stare decisis set out in Chapter 3 and above describe the view of common law courts. However, some, perhaps most U.S. Federal Circuit Court of Appeal panels take a looser view of what constitutes a holding – and consequently a looser view of stare decisis, since a looser view of what constitutes a holding loosens the force of stare decisis. Although this book concerns common law reasoning and U.S. Circuit Court of Appeal panels mostly decide constitutional and statutory cases they do decide common law cases as well, so for the sake of completeness I will now consider that view.

An example is *Pretka* v. *Kolter City Plaza II, Inc.*[17] in which an Eleventh Circuit panel declined to follow what most members of the profession probably would consider the holdings of an Eleventh Circuit precedent, *Lowery* v. *Alabama Power Co.*,[18] on the ground that the would-be holdings in *Lowery* (or, more precisely, statements that would normally be treated as holdings) were dicta:

> There are two statements in the *Lowery* opinion with which we disagree and that are at least arguably inconsistent with the result we reach in this case. The first one is that the receipt from the plaintiff rule is not limited to removals made under the second paragraph of section 1446(b) but applies to first paragraph removals as well …. That part of the opinion [statement] … is not "fitted to the facts" …, it [extended] "further than the facts of the case … and it is not "necessary to the decision" …. [A]nything the opinion says about the law applicable to cases removed under the first paragraph of section 1446(b)] is dicta, and we are "free to give that question fresh consideration." …
>
> The second statement in the *Lowery* opinion with which we disagree and that is at least arguably inconsistent with the result we reach here is the suggestion that its "receipt from the plaintiff rule would apply to any case in which the complaint seeks

[17] 608 F.3d 744 (11th Cir. 2010).
[18] 483 F.3d 1184 (11th Cir. 2007).

unliquidated damages" . . .. The *Lowery* opinion's broad statement about all complaints seeking unliquidated damages is dicta because it is unnecessary to the decision in the case.

The *Pretka* court's statements that the rules adopted in *Lowery* were not "fitted to the facts of the case," extended "further than the facts of the case," and "were unnecessary to the decision" were disingenuous because few if any holdings could escape those scythes. It's pretty clear that the *Pretka* court took its approach because as the opinion made clear the court strongly disapproved the rules adopted in *Lowery*; the rules it adopted were inconsistent with the rules adopted in *Lowery*; and under the law-of-the-Circuit doctrine the court could not reject those rules if they were holdings; so to get over that hurdle the court asserted that the rules adopted in *Lowery* were only dicta.

The approach to holdings taken in *Pretka* and by other panels that take a similar view of what constitutes a holding is not taken in all Circuits. For example, in *United States* v. *Johnson*,[19] the Ninth Circuit, sitting en banc, held that where a panel confronts an issue that is germane to the resolution of the eventual result of a case, and resolves the issue after reasoned consideration, the ruling becomes the law of the Circuit regardless of whether making it so is necessary in some strict logical sense.

---

[19] *United States* v. *Johnson*, 256 F.3d 895 (9th Cir. 2001).

5 REASONING FROM AUTHORITATIVE ALTHOUGH NOT LEGALLY BINDING RULES

The most prominent type of rules employed in American common law reasoning are rules established in legally binding precedents. The next most prominent type are authoritative although not legally binding rules. An authoritative although not legally binding rule is a rule that courts treat as a rule not because after due consideration they conclude it is the best possible rule but because the rule was adopted in a source, such as a leading treatise, to which courts give deference.

For example, the black-letter provisions of Restatements are formulated as rules, and courts frequently apply them as rules. Thus, courts will often say "under section 90 of the Restatement of Contracts ...." or "section 90 of the Restatement of Contracts provides ...," or the like. Similarly, courts treat leading treatises, such as Williston on Contracts, Corbin on Contracts, and Wigmore on Evidence, as authoritative, not merely persuasive. So too, a court will treat rules of contract law that have been adopted by many or most states and the Restatement of Contracts as law even if the court itself and many other states have not passed on the issue.[1]

Whether a source is authoritative can best be understood by considering the rule of recognition, a concept famously developed by H.L.A. Hart.[2] Hart began with the proposition that a legal system consists of a union of primary and secondary rules.

---

[1] For readers who are not members of the legal profession, every section of a Restatement is divided into three parts: the rule adopted in the section, comments on the rule, and Reporter's Notes. The rule adopted in the section is printed in bold face – hence the term *black letter*.

[2] H.L.A. HART, THE CONCEPT OF LAW (2d ed. 1994).

Primary rules are what Hart referred to as rules of obligation.[3] A more expansive definition would include rules of conduct, rules concerning rights and duties, and rules concerning how actors can make legally binding arrangements, such as contracts, wills, or transfers of property.

Secondary rules specify the ways in which primary rules may be conclusively ascertained, introduced, established, changed, applied, or eliminated, and have the fact of their violation conclusively determined.[4] Most secondary rules are legal rules – for example, legal rules concerning what constitutes a quorum for a legislative body. The most important type of secondary rule, which Hart called a rule of recognition, concerns what rules *are* legal rules. A rule of recognition is not itself a legal rule and is not established by legal rules. Rather, its force derives from the acceptance of the rule by a social group. As Dworkin observed, "The rule of recognition is the sole rule in a legal system whose binding force depends on its acceptance."[5] For example, Hart pointed out that what the Queen in Parliament enacts as law is law, but it is not law because a legal rule makes it law; it is law because a relevant social group accepts that what the Queen in Parliament enacts is law. So too is this true of why the American Constitution was law before any court treated it as law. Because a rule of recognition is a social rule the social group whose acceptance is required varies among societies. In the United States the primary group whose acceptance is required is the legal profession— judges, practicing lawyers, and legal academics. By analogy to the rule of recognition, in American common law whether a source that is not legally binding is authoritative depends on the view of the profession.

In the common law there are several sources of authoritative although not legally binding rules. One source consists of decisions by the supreme courts of other jurisdictions. As Kent Greenawalt writes:

> [If,] in respect to an issue of commercial law touching many inter-state transactions, thirty state supreme courts have gone one way and none the opposite way, the thirty-first court has a strong reason to follow prevailing doctrine even if the judges would find the opposing rule to be slightly preferable. In short, in some situations,

---

[3] *Id.* at 94.
[4] *Id.*
[5] Ronald Dworkin, The Model of Rules, 35 U. Chi. L Rev. 14, 21 (1967)

a court that is not "bound" according to traditional doctrine has grounds for following the rules of precedents that go beyond the persuasiveness of their reasoning.

... A court does not violate any traditional sense of the force of precedent if it relies on what it takes as sufficiently strong reasons to decide contrary to what the previous courts (below it or outside the jurisdiction) have held. But if a court paid no attention to these prior rulings or assigned no weight at all to the reasons for following them, it would not act responsibly.[6]

Greenawalt's analysis is exemplified by *McIntyre* v. *Ballentine*, decided by the Tennessee Supreme Court.[7] *McIntyre* involved the problem, what result if a defendant negligently injures a plaintiff but the plaintiff's own negligence contributed to her injury? Under one approach, known as contributory negligence, the plaintiff's negligence bars her from recovery. Under a competing approach, known as comparative negligence, the plaintiff's recovery is reduced by reason of her negligence but she is not barred from recovery. For a long period of time the doctrine of contributory negligence was almost universally adopted. Gradually, however, courts adopted various forms of comparative negligence instead. As of 1992 Tennessee was one of the few states that still followed the doctrine of contributory negligence. In *McIntyre* the plaintiff was injured as a result of the defendant's negligence but the plaintiff was also negligent. The trial court instructed the jury on the basis of the contributory negligence rule, and the jury found for the defendant. The Tennessee Supreme Court reversed, relying in part on the fact that comparative negligence had replaced contributory negligence in forty-five other states.

Another source of authoritative although not binding rules consists of cases decided by coordinate courts, such as courts of intermediate appeals in the same jurisdiction as the deciding court.

Dicta are another source of authoritative although not legally binding rules. For example, a Federal District Court or Court of Appeal will normally treat strong dicta of the United States Supreme Court as rules even though they are not binding. As Judge Frank Easterbrook said, "The Supreme Court often articulates positions through language that

---

[6] KENT GREENAWALT, STATUTORY AND COMMON LAW INTERPRETATION 199–200 (2013).
[7] 853 S.W.2d 52 (1992).

an unsympathetic audience might dismiss as dictum ... and it expects those formulations to be followed."[8]

Still other, very important sources of authoritative although not legally binding rules are Restatements and leading treatises.

While authoritative although not legally binding rules impose no legal obligation such rules often have as much or even more power as legally binding rules, and cases are commonly decided on the basis of rules found in Restatements or leading treatises. *Cukor* v. *Mikalauskas*, discussed in Chapter 1, is an example. A more powerful example is the principle of reliance in contract law. Prior to 1932, generally speaking reliance had little role to play in contract law. Under the bargain principle of consideration, with limited exceptions only bargain promises were enforceable, and a promisee's reliance on a nonbargain promise – in particular a donative promise, that is, a promise to make a gift, did not make the promise enforceable. So Holmes said, "It would cut up the doctrine of consideration by the roots, if a promisee could make a gratuitous promise enforceable by subsequently acting in reliance on it."[9]

This principle was exemplified in *Kirksey* v. *Kirksey*.[10] Antillico was a widow with several children. She resided on public land sixty or seventy miles away from her brother-in-law, Kirksey. In October 1840, Kirksey wrote to Antillico as follows:

> Dear Sister Antillico, —Much to my mortification I heard that brother Henry was dead, and one of his children. I know that your situation is one of grief and difficulty. You had a bad chance before, but a great deal worse now. ... If you will come down and see me, I will let you have a place to raise your family, and I have more open land than I can tend; and on the account of your situation, and that of your family, I feel like I want you and the children to do well.

Soon after receipt of this letter, Antillico abandoned her possession and moved with her family to Kirksey's premises. For two years Kirksey put her in a comfortable house and gave her land to tend. Thereafter he put

---

[8] *United States* v. *Bloom*, 149 F.2d 649 (7th Cir. 1998).
[9] *Commonwealth* v. *Scituate Savings Bank*, 137 Mass. 301, 302 (1884).
[10] 8 Ala. 131 (1845).

her in a different house, not comfortable, in the woods. Later, he
required her to leave his premises entirely.

Anitllico then sued Kirksey for breach of contract. The trial court
rendered a verdict in her favor for $200, and Kirksey appealed. The
Alabama Supreme Court reversed. The opinion was written by Judge
Ormond, who dissented from the reversal:

> The inclination of my mind is that the loss and inconvenience
> which the plaintiff sustained in breaking up and moving to the
> defendant's a distance of sixty miles is a sufficient consideration
> to support the plaintiff's promise to furnish her with a house and
> land to cultivate until she could raise her family. My brothers,
> however, think that [Kirksey's] promise was a mere gratuity, and
> that an action will not lie for its breach.

So matters more or less stood until the publication of the authoritative
although not legally binding Restatement of Contracts in 1932.
Section 90 of that Restatement provided that a promise that the prom-
iser should reasonably expect to induce action or forbearance on the
part of the promisee and that does induce such action or forbearance is
binding if injustice can be avoided only by enforcement of the promise.

Based on section 90 the courts now almost universally hold that
a relied-upon donative promise is enforceable. Even more striking, the
reliance principle embodied in section 90 swept through contract law,
impacting such areas as the law of offer and acceptance,[11] mistake,[12]
remedies,[13] and the Statute of Frauds.[14] In short, the authoritative
although not legally binding principle of section 90 has had an impact
on contract law much greater than most legally binding rules.[15]

---

[11] *See Drennan* v. *Star Paving Co.*, 333 P.2d 757 (Cal. 1958); RESTATEMENT OF CONTRACTS §
87(2).

[12] *See* RESTATEMENT OF CONTRACTS § 135, comment d.

[13] *See* RESTATEMENT OF CONTRACTS § 349.

[14] *See* RESTATEMENT OF CONTRACTS § 139.

[15] Prior to the adoption of section 90 there was a handful of specific categories in which
reliance made a promise enforceable. However, those categories were not based on and did
not recognize a general principle that reliance made a promise enforceable. More important section 90, although loosely supported by those categories, was principally based on
what the law should be. It was only as a result of section 90 that contract law adopted
a general principle that reliance made a promise enforceable, and it was only as a result of
section 90 that the reliance principle swept through contract law.

Similarly, from the 1940s through the 1970s, contract law was dominated by great multivolume treatises authored by Samuel Williston of Harvard Law School and Arthur Corbin of Yale Law School. These and certain other treatises were frequently cited by courts in the same way as binding precedents. Here is an excerpt from *Contemporary Mission* v. *Famous Music Corp.*[16] that illustrates the force of leading treatises in legal reasoning:[17]

> There is no dispute that the sale of Famous' record division to ABC constituted an assignment of the Crunch agreement to ABC. The assignment of a bilateral contract includes both an assignment of rights and a delegation of duties. See 3 Williston on Contracts § 418 (3d ed. 1960). The distinctions between the two are important.
>
> Perhaps more frequently than is the case with other terms of art, lawyers seem prone to use the word "assignment" inartfully, frequently intending to encompass within the term the distinct (concept) of delegation . . .. An assignment involves the transfer of rights. A delegation involves the appointment of another to perform one's duties. J. Calamari & J. Perillo, Contracts § 254 (1970). . . .
>
> It is true, of course, as a general rule, that when rights are assigned, the assignor's interest in the rights assigned comes to an end. When duties are delegated, however, the delegant's obligation does not end. . . . "No one can assign his liabilities under a contract without the consent of the party to whom he is liable. This is sufficiently obvious when attention is called to it, for otherwise obligors would find an easy practical way of escaping their obligations . . .." 3 Williston on Contracts § 411 (3d ed. 1960).

The role of authoritative although not legally binding rules in legal reasoning is forcefully illustrated by the data. A study of opinions in sixteen state supreme courts during 1940–70 found that unofficial sources, primarily Restatements, treatises, and law reviews, were cited in almost half the opinions.[18] The same study found that citations

---

[16] 557 F.2d 918 (2d Cir. 1977).

[17] *Contemporary Mission* is discussed at greater length in Chapter 8.

[18] L. Friedman, R. Kagan, B. Cartwright & S. Wheeler, *State Supreme Courts: A Century of Style and Citation*, 33 STAN. L. REV. 773, 796–808, 810–16 (1981).

to out-of-state cases accounted for about a quarter of all citations to
state cases. More impressively the ALI's Restatements and Principles
of Law were cited more than 2,700 times by state and federal courts in
the one-year period July 2019–June 2020, and the total number of
citations to Restatements and Principles of Law as of June 2020 was
over 213,000.[19]

---

[19] Email from Megan Dingley of the ALI to Melvin A. Eisenberg, August 5, 2020. These
numbers represent total citations, not the number of court opinions containing such
citations. For example, a single case could contain citations to three different sections of
RESTATEMENT (THIRD) OF AGENCY and this will count as three citations for the purposes of
the ALI's data. On the other hand, the reported citations are limited to those gathered from
opinions published in West's National Reporter System Reporters. *Id.*

6 THE ROLE OF MORAL, POLICY, AND EMPIRICAL PROPOSITIONS IN LEGAL REASONING, AND THE JUDICIAL ADOPTION OF NEW LEGAL RULES BASED ON SOCIAL PROPOSITIONS

The common law is based on doctrinal and social propositions. Doctrinal propositions are propositions that purport to state legal rules and are found in sources that in the view of the legal profession – judges, practicing lawyers, and legal academics – state legal doctrine. *Social propositions* are comprised of moral, policy, and empirical propositions. The two types of propositions do very different work. Doctrinal propositions are legal rules. Social propositions are the reasons for legal rules.

To put this differently, social propositions provide the justification of legal rules. Justification in the common law takes two forms: the justification for *following* a rule and the justification *of* a rule. In the common law a court is justified in following a rule if the rule is established in a binding legal precedent decided by a superior court or by the same court. However, the fact that a rule is established in a binding legal precedent does not justify the rule. Rather, a common-law rule is justified only if it is supported by social propositions. I will refer to legal rules that are justified by social propositions as rules that are congruent with social propositions.

This chapter considers the roles of moral, policy, and empirical propositions in legal reasoning.

MORALITY

Moral propositions characterize conduct as right or wrong, good or bad, fair or unfair, just or unjust, faulty or fault-free. These propositions play a significant role in fashioning important areas of American common law, such as the law of torts, and important parts of the law of contracts, as well as specific rules and the decisions of individual cases.

When morality is relevant to legal reasoning an important issue is what kinds of moral propositions common law courts employ. For purposes of this issue moral propositions fall into three categories: the judge's personal morality, critical morality, and social morality.

The Judge's Personal Morality

There are good reasons why the judge's personal morality does not figure in common law reasoning. To begin with, because courts are largely removed from ordinary political processes the legitimacy of judicial decision making and lawmaking in the common law depends in large part on the employment of a process of reasoning that begins with legal rules and the society's standards rather than the standards that a judge thinks best.

Next, in the vast majority of cases in which law becomes important to a private actor, as a practical matter the institution that determines the law for the actor is not a court but a lawyer. It is therefore important that courts use a process of legal reasoning that is replicable by lawyers, so that lawyers involved in planning and dispute settlement can give reliable advice about the law.

In short, the use of replicable modes of legal reasoning by the courts serves as an instrumentality that allows private actors to make individual and joint plans and settle disputes without going to courts – and personal morality is not replicable. So as Cardozo said, "The judge ... is not a knight-errant, roaming at will in pursuit of his own ideal of beauty or goodness. He is to draw his inspiration from consecrated principles."[1]

[1] Benjamin Cardozo, The Nature of the Judicial Process 141 (1931).

Critical Morality

Critical morality can be defined in various ways. H.L.A. Hart defined it to mean "the general moral principles used in criticism of actual social institutions including positive morality"[2] (by which he meant "the morality actually shared and accepted by a given social group"[3]) or the "forms of enlightened moral criticism urged by individuals whose moral horizon has transcended the morality currently accepted."[4] An alternative definition of critical morality is standards of right and wrong that are established by critical analysis without regard to whether the standards have support in the community. Critical morality is not employed in legal reasoning, partly because there are many schools of critical morality and any school would only accidentally, if at all, reflect the society's morality, and partly because normally legal reasoning based on critical morality could not be replicated by lawyers because lawyers could not easily know which school of critical morality a judge adhered to.

Social or Conventional Morality

Social or conventional morality can also be described in various ways. Hart employed several definitions, including positive morality,[5] accepted social morality,[6] and conventional morality.[7] Larry Alexander and Emily Sherman refer to the moral values to which the community agrees at a fairy high level of generality and which members of the community accept as guides for their own action.[8] Another definition, used in this book, is moral norms that are rooted in aspirations for the community as a whole and have substantial support in the community. Under any of these definitions, when morality is relevant to deciding a case or making law the reason courts employ social morality is the converse of the reason why they do not employ personal

[2] H.L.A. HART, LAW, LIBERTY AND MORALITY 20 (1963).
[3] Id.
[4] H.L.A. HART, THE CONCEPT OF LAW 185 (2d ed. 1994).
[5] Id.
[6] Id. at 204.
[7] Id. at 169, 200.
[8] LARRY ALEXANDER & EMILY SHERWIN, DEMYSTIFYING LEGAL REASONING 9 (2008).

morality. First, courts, which are usually unelected and politically unaccountable, draw their legitimacy from adherence to legal rules and social standards. Second, because social morality is objective and observable the employment of social morality makes legal reasoning replicable by the profession in a way that a judge's personal morality and critical morality do not.

I turn now to two areas of common law, torts and contracts, that center almost entirely or in significant part on social morality.

Tort Law

The rules of tort law are largely based on social morality, in particular fault, with some additional rules based on social policy. As stated in Dobbs, Hayden, and Bublick's *Hornbook on Torts*, ":[T]orts are traditionally associated with wrongdoing in some moral sense."[9] ...[T]ort law attempts to recognize personal responsibility and accountability for harms done to others. It does so primarily by allocating some or all responsibility to those who are at fault. The issue of fault thus dominates most of tort law."[10]

Contract Law

In contrast to tort law, which is largely based on social morality with additional rules based on social policy, contract law is largely based on social policy with additional rules based on social morality. The basic social policy on which contract law rests is that the facilitation and enforcement of bargains is socially desirable. Many specific rules of contract law are also based on policies. For example, a promise that is unreasonably in restraint of trade is unenforceable on the ground of public policy.[11] So is a promise that is in restraint of marriage, detrimental to the marriage relationship, affects custody, involves the commission of a tort, induces violation of a fiduciary duty, interferes with

---

[9] DAN B. DOBBS, DAVID T. HAYDEN & ELLEN M. BUBICK, HORNBOOK ON TORTS 4 (2d ed. 2016).
[10] *Id.* at 12.
[11] RESTATEMENT OF CONTRACTS section 186.

a contract with another, or exempts liability for harm caused intentionally or recklessly.[12]

Given the strong policy reasons for facilitating and enforcing bargains it is not surprising that under the school of thought now known as
classical contract law, which prevailed from around the middle of the
nineteenth century to the early part of the twentieth, moral considerations were largely absent from contract law, and under the bargain
principle bargains were enforceable according to their terms with little
or no room for consideration of fairness. Under modern contract law,
in contrast, while the facilitation and enforcement of bargains remains
central, three fundamental areas, and many rules outside those areas,
turn on social morality. The areas are reliance, unconscionability, and
good faith.

Reliance

Under the bargain principle as it figured in classical contract law, with
very limited exceptions only bargain promises were enforceable. As
a corollary, with very limited exceptions a promisee's unbargained-for
reliance on a promise did not make the promise enforceable. This rule
was morally unjustified, because a promisor who makes a promise that
it can reasonably foresee the promisee will rely on is at fault for making
the promise and then breaking it after the promisee has incurred costs it
would not have otherwise incurred, on the reasonable assumption that
the promise would be kept. Because this rule was incongruent with
social morality and unsupported by policy it was inevitable that it would
be overthrown. The overthrow began in 1932 with the publication of
Restatement of Contracts section 90, discussed in Chapter 5. As
applied to the enforceability of promises section 90 is commonly
referred to as the principle of promissory estoppel.

Section 90 was not law, but as a provision of the Restatement of
Contracts it was authoritative, and since the adoption of section 90
reliance has become an embedded principle of American contract law.
Indeed, because of the moral force of the reliance principle its application has spread to areas of contract law beyond the enforceability of

---

[12] *Id.* sections 187–95.

promises, including remedies, mistake, unexpected circumstances, offer and acceptance, and the Statute of Frauds.

Unconscionability

Another important development in modern contract law is the emergence of the principle that an unconscionable contract is unenforceable. Unconscionability is a moral concept – not conscionable means not in accord with good moral conscience or seriously unfair. Unconscionability was not a recognized principle under classical contract law. On the contrary, under the bargain principle bargains were enforceable according to their terms, without regard to fairness. Beginning in the 1960s, however, the position of contract law changed fundamentally under the impetus of Uniform Commercial Code (UCC) section 2-302, which provides that in contracts for the sale of goods if the court as a matter of law finds the contract or any clause of the contract to be unconscionable at the time it was made the court may refuse to enforce the contract, or it may enforce the remainder of the contract without the unconscionability clause, or it may so limit the application of any unconscionable clause as to avoid any unconscionable result.

The UCC is a statute, not part of the common law. However, just as Restatement of Contracts section 90 was not law but was authoritative and the principle it embodied swept through contract law, so too the principle of unconscionability embodied in section 2-302 swept through contract law.

The principle of unconscionability is too general to apply directly to decide most cases. Instead, the importance of the principle is that it can generate specific rules that can be directly applied. Among these rules are the following:

• A prohibition on unfair surprise, which occurs where a party, A, inserts into a contract a provision that disadvantages A's counterparty, B, and A knows or should know that the provision lies outside B's reasonable expectation, B will probably not notice the provision, and B is unlikely to understand the provision if she does notice it;
• A prohibition on price-gouging, in which a seller takes advantage of a temporary disruption of a market, such as a blackout or an earthquake,

to charge a price well above the prevailing market price prior to the disruption;
• A prohibition on the exploitation of transactional incapacity, in which A exploits B's lack of aptitude, experience, or judgmental ability to make a well-informed decision concerning the desirability of a complex bargain.

———————

The Duty of Good Faith

A third principle of contract law that rests on social morality is the duty of good faith – *good faith* here being a surrogate term for *in a morally proper manner*. The duty is stated in Restatement Second of Contracts section 205: "Every contract imposes upon each party a duty of good faith and fair dealing in its performance and its enforcement."

This duty is manifested in various ways. For example, in *Market Street Associates Ltd. Partnership* v. *Frey*,[13] Judge Posner held that a party to a contract is under a duty of good faith not to take advantage of an obvious oversight by its counterparty concerning the provisions of the contract. In *Greer Properties, Inc.* v. *LaSalle National Bank*[14] a contract for the sale of real estate to Greer included a provision that required the seller to clean up environmental waste on the property unless the clean-up turned out to be economically impracticable. The seller then retained a soil consultant who provided a fairly low estimate for the clean up. Thereafter, the seller terminated the contract under the clean-up provision and made a new contract with a third party who agreed to pay a higher price than Greer had agreed to pay. The court held that it would violate the duty of good faith for the seller to invoke the clean-up provision where its real purpose for terminating the contract with Greer was to sell the property at a higher price.

———————

In addition to these three broad areas of contract law social morality figures in a variety of more specific rules. For example, if A begins to perform services that will benefit B, A and B have not made a contract concerning those services, but B knows or has reason to know that

---

[13] 941 F.2d 588 (7th Cir. 1991).
[14] 874 F.2d 467 (7th Cir. 1989).

A expects to be paid for the services and B can with little trouble inform A that he will not pay, then as a matter of fairness B should so inform A. Accordingly, the rule in such cases is that B is liable for the value of A's services if he stays silent.[15] Similarly, suppose Seller's salesperson solicits an offer from Buyer for goods, subject to Seller's acceptance. Seller knows or should know that Buyer will be unable to purchase comparable goods from a third party while it awaits word from Seller, because if Seller accepts Buyer's offer Buyer would have an oversupply of the goods. Under these circumstances Buyer will have a reasonable expectation, created by Seller, that Seller will notify Buyer if it does not intend to accept the offer that Seller's salesperson solicited. Therefore, as a matter of fairness Seller should give Buyer notice if it does not intend to accept the offer, or be held liable on a contract based on the terms of the offer. That is indeed the rule.[16]

Legal Positivism

In considering the role of morality in legal reasoning account needs to be taken of the school of thought known as legal positivism. H.L.A. Hart is the leading modern legal positivist, and I will focus on his views. A central claim of legal positivism is that there is a separation between law and morals. Indeed, this was the centerpiece of Hart's well-known article *Positivism and the Separation of Law and Morals*.[17] If the title of Hart's article is taken literally it is clearly incorrect, because as shown above morality plays important roles in at least two great bodies of American common law, torts and contracts. However, Hart's title should not be taken literally because Hart agreed that morality plays a significant role in the law. So, for example, in *The Concept of Law* Hart stated:

> [I]t cannot be seriously disputed that the development of law, at all times and places, has in fact been profoundly influenced both by the conventional morality and ideals of particular social groups, and also by forms of enlightened moral criticism urged by individuals, whose moral horizon has transcended the morality currently accepted. . . .

[15] *See, e.g., Day* v. *Caton*, 119 Mass. 513 (1876).
[16] *See, e.g., Ammns* v. *Wilson & Co.*, 170 So. 227 (Miss. 1936).
[17] H.L.A. Hart, Positivism and the Separation of Law and Morals, 71 Harv. L. Rev. 595 (1958).

The law of every modern state shows at a thousand points the influence of both the accepted social morality and wider moral ideals. These influences enter into law either abruptly and avowedly through legislation, or silently and piecemeal through the judicial process. . . .

The . . . ways in which law mirrors morality are myriad. . . .

No "positivist" could deny that these are the facts or that the stability of legal systems depends in part upon such types of correspondence with morals. If this is what is meant by the necessary connection of law and morals, its existence should be conceded.[18]

It is tempting to stop here and conclude that there is no inconsistency between legal positivism, as exemplified by Hart, and the view that many legal rules are based on morality – after all, that is just what Hart said. However, this would not adequately account for Hart's views (and more generally the views of legal positivism) on law and morality, because those views include two important tenets concerning the relation between law and morality that also need to be considered.

The first tenet is that the validity of a legal rule does not depend on whether the rule conforms to morality. This tenet is certainly true of statutes, at least if we put to one side outliers like many of the statutes adopted in Hitler's Third Reich, but it is not invariably true of American common law. Most common law rules are likely to be supported by social morality, social policy, or both at the time of their inception. However, social propositions may evolve over time, and often they evolve in such a way that a rule that was supported by social propositions at its inception comes to gradually lose that support. A rule that loses such support is unsound and a candidate for overruling, and the continued validity of such a rule is doubtful even before it is explicitly overruled. (I do not claim that legal rules must be moral or that moral rules are part of the legal system. Far from it: statutory rules are normally valid even if immoral and moral rules, as such, are not legal rules. For example, it is a basic moral principle that one should keep one's promises, but a promise, as such, is not legally enforceable.)

Hart's second tenet was that there is a sharp distinction in the law between ought and is. Now of course ought and is are different concepts. However, in American common law ought often morphs into is,

[18] H.L.A. HART, THE CONCEPT OF LAW 185, 203–04 (2d ed. 1994).

just as a child morphs into an adult. And just as it is often difficult to say when a child has become an adult so too it is often difficult to say when ought has become is in American common law.

Take, for example, the reliance principle in contract law, discussed above. Prior to 1932 it could fairly be said that foreseeable reliance on a promise *ought* to make the promise enforceable but it could not be said that foreseeable reliance on a promise *did* make a promise enforceable. However, after the adoption of Restatement of Contracts section 90 in 1932, followed by the almost universal recognition of the principle of promissory estoppel, the teaching in every law school that promissory estoppel was law, and the black-letter statements in treatises that foreseeable reliance made a promise enforceable, the principle that foreseeable reliance on a promise *ought* to make a promise enforceable gradually morphed into the principle that foreseeable reliance *does* make a promise enforceable, even in states where the courts had not had occasion to so rule. To put it differently, well-informed and capable lawyers in a state that had not yet had occasion to pass on the issue would surely advise their clients that today foreseeable reliance makes a promise enforceable even though no case had so held in their state.

Or take the principle of unconscionability. Prior to 1962 it could fairly be said that unconscionability *ought* to make a contract unenforceable, but it could not be said that unconscionability *did* make a contract unenforceable. However, after the adoption of UCC section 2-302 in 1962 the concept that an unconscionable contract is unenforceable, having been adopted in many states, taught in all law schools, and stated as law in treatises, gradually morphed into the principle that an unconscionable contract is unenforceable.

So, whatever is the case with statutes, in American common law – which is, after all, law – the tenet that there is invariably a sharp distinction between ought and is in the law is inaccurate as a generalization.

Why did Hart and other legal positivists not see that, as evidenced by American common law, in a given legal system ought could morph into is; the point at which the metamorphosis occurred could be difficult to determine; and legal rules could depend for their continued existence, and therefore their continued validity, on their congruence with social morality? Perhaps this was because Hart was not intimately acquainted with American common law and American common law reasoning. Also, England has no counterpart to the Restatements, English common law courts do not seem to give the same deference to legal treatises as American common law courts, and England is a unitary jurisdiction, so that there is no counterpart in England to the way in which Restatements, leading treatises, and cases in multiple jurisdictions frequently move American common law from ought to is.[19]

Then, too as Jules Coleman and Brian Leiter point out, "[f]or the positivist, the central figure is the lawmaker or legislator rather than the judge."[20]

POLICIES

In contrast to moral norms, which characterize conduct as right or wrong, good or bad, fair or unfair, just or unjust, policies characterize states of affairs as conducive or adverse to public welfare. *Social policies* are policies that have substantial support in the community or, in the absence of explicit support, policies which there is reason to conclude would command substantial support if the question was put.

Social policies figure heavily in common law reasoning because when a court makes a new rule or modifies an existing rule it must often take into account whether the new or modified rule would be conducive or adverse to public welfare. And just as when the courts base legal rules on morality they employ social morality, so too where courts base rules on policies they employ social policies.

How do courts determine social morality or social policy? To begin with, judges are almost invariably experienced members of their society, and know what policies have substantial social support or would have such support if the community explicitly addressed the relevant

[19] There is a statutory British Law Commission, but its major function is to advise Parliament on such matters as repealing obsolete enactments, streamlining over-complicated law, and formulating new statutory approaches to high-profile social issues. See The Law Commission, THE WORK OF THE LAW COMMISSION.
[20] Jules Coleman & Brian Leiter, *Legal Positivism, in A COMPANION TO LEGAL THEORY* 228, 229 (Dennis Patterson ed., 2d ed. 2010).

issue. Next, judgments on what constitutes social morality or social policy are not confined to the narrow arena of individual judicial decisions. Instead, they are also subject to criticism in the discourse in wider arenas, in decisions by sister courts, in meetings of professional organizations, and in law review articles and legal treatises. If a court gets social morality or social policy wrong criticism in these arenas is likely to confine the court's view to a single decision.

It is true that society is highly divided on some moral issues, such as abortion, and some policy issues, such as mandatory vaccination. However, highly divisive issues, such as those, rarely figure in the common law. Rather, the common law is largely concerned with issues that are either relatively clear or low-key, such as whether it is morally wrong to intentionally or negligently injure another or to defame another or whether it is good policy to enforce bargains.

I will focus on the role of social policy in contract and tort law. As shown above much or most of contract law is based on social policy. So are several areas of tort law. One area concerns conduct in the course of litigation. As stated in Dobbs, Hayden, and Bublick's *Hornbook on Torts*:

> Almost everyone directly involved in litigation enjoys an absolute immunity for communications made in the litigation or even in preparation for it lest the voices of the honest be stilled by fear of liability. Beyond that, judges are immune from suit based on their rulings in a case over which they have jurisdiction, even if the ruling is erroneous or malicious. ... [W]itnesses are immune [with a limited exception in some states concerning expert witnesses]; even those who testify to a knowing falsehood avoid liability to those harmed by his testimony . . .. Official prosecutors, grand juries, and those in similar roles are absolutely immune for their decision to prosecute as well as for their in-trial conduct.[21]

Various rules of strict (non-fault) liability in the law of torts are also based on social policy. These include principals' vicarious liability for torts committed by their agents in the course of their employment,[22] strict liability for injuries caused by pets who are abnormally dangerous

---

[21] DAN B. DOBBS, PAUL T. HAYDEN & ELLEN M. BUBICK, HORNBOOK ON TORTS 1024–25 (2016).
[22] *Id.* at 73–75.

as their owner knows,[23] and strict liability for injuries caused by a wild animal kept by a private owner.[24]

In addition to general areas, such as litigation immunity and vicarious and strict liability, many individual tort-law decisions are based on policy. For example, in *Vasilenko* v. *Grace Family Church*,[25] decided by the California Supreme Court, Vasilenko was injured when he crossed a street midblock between his church and the church's overflow parking lot. He sued the church on the ground that it owed parishioners a duty to warn them of the danger posed by crossing the street to the overflow parking lot, and was negligent in failing to do so. Section 714 of the California Civil Code established a general duty of each person to exercise in his or her activities reasonable care for the safety of others. The Court began by referring to this section but added that courts should create exceptions where clearly supported by public policy and concluded that public policy supported an exception in this case:

> Vasilenko ... contends that landowners can warn of the danger of crossing the street, perhaps by posting a sign. But the danger posed by crossing a public street midblock is obvious, and there is ordinarily no duty to warn of obvious dangers. ... Although some fraction of people may fail to appreciate an obvious danger, "to require warnings for the sake of such persons would produce such a profusion of warnings as to devalue those warnings serving a more important function." (Rest.3d Torts, Liability for Physical and Emotional Harm, § 18, com. f, p. 208)...

> We must also account for the possibility that finding a duty in this case will cause some or perhaps many landowners to stop providing parking. ... Although landowners are not required to provide parking for their invitees, it is often socially desirable for landowners to do so. Providing parking reduces traffic and its associated dangers. Drivers looking for parking may pay less attention to other hazards than they otherwise would. They may also disrupt the flow of traffic by driving more slowly than other drivers, by stopping periodically to wait for parking spaces to free up, or by speeding up suddenly to capture an available space. By providing parking, a landowner may

[23] *See id.* at 779–80.
[24] See RESTATEMENT OF TORTS section 22.
[25] 3 Cal.5th 1077, 1088, 1090. (2017).

decrease its invitees' risk of injury from other dangers of the road as compared to invitees finding their own parking on the streets.

Similarly, in *Gregory* v. *Cott*[26] Cott was a violent Alzheimer's patient whose husband maintained her at home with a caregiver, Gregory, rather than institutionalizing her. During a struggle Cott cut Gregory badly with a knife, and Gregory brought suit against Cott and her husband. Under California law Alzheimer's patients were not liable for injuries caused to caregivers in institutional settings, but there was no counterpart rule on injuries Alzheimer's patients caused to home caregivers. The court held for the Cotts because "California public policy clearly favors alternative arrangements in which these patients are assisted to remain at home. The contemporary view of institutionalization as a last resort counsels in favor of a rule that encourages families to retain trained home health care workers to supervise and assist late-stage Alzheimer's patients."

Again it is true that society is highly divided on some moral issues, such as abortion, and some policy issues, such as mandatory vaccination. However, highly divisive issues do not often figure in the common law. Rather, the common law is largely concerned with relatively clear or low-key moral and policy issues, such as whether it is morally bad to intentionally or negligently injure or defame a person, whether is good policy to enforce bargains, or whether it is bad policy to adopt a rule that would likely result in families institutionalizing Alzheimer's patients rather than caring for them at home.

Despite the overpowering reasons why courts should consider policies in establishing or revising common law rules, and the widespread employment of policies in the common law, Ronald Dworkin claimed that "judicial decisions in civil cases characteristically ... should be generated by principle not policy."[27] Dworkin rested this claim on three arguments.

First, Dworkin argued that as an empirical matter "judicial decisions in civil cases ... are characteristically ... guided by principle not

[26] 39 Cal.4th 1112. (2006).
[27] Ronald Dworkin, Hard Cases, 88 HARV. L. REV. 1057, 1060, 1063 (1973).

policy,"[28] by which presumably he meant moral principles. As shown above, this claim is incorrect; an overpowering number of common law rules and cases rest on social policy.

Second, Dworkin argued that a community should be governed by individuals who are elected by and responsible to the majority, and since judges are for the most part not elected and not responsible to the electorate judges should not make law.[29] This argument is flawed. The fact that an institution is composed of persons who are elected and responsible to the majority is one source of legitimacy but it is not the only source. That an institution serves the public interest is another source of legitimacy and in making private law courts do just that. Moreover, making courts take account of social policies is not undesirable; what would be undesirable is for courts *not* to take account of social policies. Finally, if judges should not make law then the common law would have to be wiped off the books, because it is made by judges.

Third, Dworkin argued that "if a judge makes new law and applies it retroactively to the case before him, then the losing party will be punished, not because of some duty he had, but because of a duty created after the event."[30] This argument is misconceived because almost all new common law rules are retroactive.

EMPIRICAL PROPOSITIONS

Several types of empirical proposition play a role in common law reasoning. One type consists of judicial observations concerning human behavior, as in the rule that spouses cannot testify against each other. Another consists of judicial predictions concerning the effect of adopting or not adopting a given rule. Empirical propositions also often underlie social policies. For example, in contract law the policy in favor of facilitating and enforcing bargains is based on the empirical propositions that bargains create gains through trade and that the enforcement of bargains facilitates planning. Similarly, in tort law the absolute immunity for communications made in litigation is largely

---

[28] *Id.*
[29] *Id.*
[30] *Id.* at 1061.

based on the prediction that in the absence of absolute immunity honest voices would be stilled for fear of liability.

Next, empirical observations and predictions are employed by courts to reach a conclusion that a rule would be either good or bad. For example, recall that in *Vasilenko v. Grace Family Church* Vasilenko was injured when he crossed a street midblock from his church to the church's overflow parking lot. He sued the church on the ground that it was negligent in failing to warn parishioners of the danger posed by crossing the street to the parking lot. The court rejected Vasilenko's argument on the basis of social policies that it supported by empirical observations and predictions. The court first made the empirical observation that the danger in crossing the street was obvious and most people would appreciate the danger. It then made the empirical prediction that to require a warning for the sake of the few people who would not appreciate the danger would produce such a profusion of warnings as to devalue those warnings that serve a more important function. The court also predicted that imposing a duty on landowners to exercise care in such cases could result in significant burdens because landowners that wanted to provide parking would have to make difficult determinations of the availability and relative safety of parking lots, would have to continuously monitor the dangerousness of street crossings and might also need to hire employees to assist invitees with crossing the street, and these burdens could undesirably deter landowners from providing parking.

Similarly, in *Gregory v. Cott*,[31] the court held that dangerous Alzheimer's patients should not be liable for injuries they inflicted on home caregivers, based on the prediction that the imposition of liability would discourage family members from hiring home caregivers for their loved ones rather than institutionalizing them, which would be undesirable because as a matter of social policy home care is favored over institutionalization.

As evidenced by *Vasilenko* and *Cott*, courts typically provide little or no evidence for their observations and predictions, either because they

[31] 59 Cal.4th 996 (2014).

do not realize that they are relying on unproven facts or because they regard their observations and predictions as self-evident.

The Judicial Adoption of New Legal Rules

Three types of rules figure in rule-based legal reasoning in the common law. Two of these types have been considered in earlier chapters: rules established in binding legal precedents (Chapter 2) and authoritative although not binding rules (Chapter 5). The third type consists of new rules adopted by the courts on the basis of social propositions.

Hadley v. *Baxendale*, discussed in Chapter 4, is a leading example of such a rule. The issue in *Hadley* was, in the case of damages for breach of contract what must be the connection between the breach and the damages to be awarded? Prior to *Hadley* the test was whether the damages were the natural and necessary consequences of the breach or were instead too remote from the breach. In *Hadley* the court adopted a new and different rule: whether the damages were such as may fairly and reasonably be considered either arising naturally, i.e., according to the usual course of things, from such breach of contract itself, or such as may reasonably be supposed to have been in the contemplation of both parties at the time they made the contract, as the probable result of the breach of it. The court adopted this rule on the basis of an empirical proposition: That had the special circumstances of the parties been known, they might have specially provided for the breach of contract by special terms as to the damages in that case, and of this advantage it would be very unjust to deprive them.

Another example of the judicial adoption of a new legal rule based on social propositions concerns the doctrine of comparative negligence. Until the mid-twentieth century, the virtually universal rule known as contributory negligence was that if a plaintiff who had been injured as a result of a defendant's negligence was also negligent, the plaintiff was barred from bringing suit. A number of state legislatures replaced contributory negligence with comparative negligence, under which the plaintiff is not barred but has its recovery reduced in proportion to its comparative fault. That principle was then judicially adopted in *Hoffman* v. *Jones*,[32] decided by the Florida Supreme Court in 1973:

> . . .One of the most pressing social problems facing us today is the automobile accident problem, for the bulk of tort litigation involves the dangerous instrumentality known as the automobile. Our society must be concerned with accident prevention and compensation of victims of accidents. . . . The prevention of accidents, of course, is much more satisfying than the compensation of victims, but we must recognize the problem of determining a method of securing just and adequate compensation of accident victims who have a good cause of action.
>
> The contemporary conditions must be met with contemporary standards which are realistic and better calculated to obtain justice among all of the parties involved, based upon the circumstances applying between them at the time in question. The rule of contributory negligence as a complete bar to recovery was imported into the law by judges. Whatever may have been the historical justification for it, today it is almost universally regarded as unjust and inequitable to vest an entire accidental loss on one of the parties whose negligent conduct combined with the negligence of the other party to produce the loss. If fault is to remain the test of liability, then the doctrine of comparative negligence which involves apportionment of the loss among those whose fault contributed to the occurrence is more consistent with liability based on a fault premise. . . .
>
> One reason for the abandonment of the contributory negligence theory is that the initial justification for establishing the complete defense is no longer valid. . . . Modern economic and social customs . . . favor the individual, not industry.
>
> We find that none of the justifications for denying any recovery to a plaintiff, who has contributed to his own injuries to any extent, has any validity in this age.[33]

Among other new legal rules adopted by the courts on the basis of social propositions is the right of privacy, beginning with *Pavesich* v. *New England Life Ins. Co.*,[34] decided by the Georgia Supreme

[32] 280 So.2d 431, 436-37 (Fla. 1973).
[33] Id. At 436-437
[34] 122 Ga. 190 (1905).

Court in 1905 and *Kunz* v. *Allen*,[35] decided by the Kansas Supreme Court in 1918, and eventually adopted by courts throughout the United States. Still other new rules adopted by the courts on the basis of social propositions are the implied warranty of fitness by builders of new homes,[36] and the warranty of habitability by landlords who lease apartments.[37] More broadly much or all of the common law consists of rules that were once newly adopted by courts on the basis of social morality, social policy, and experience.

[35] 102 Kan. 883 (1918).
[36] *See, e.g., Waggoner* v. *Midwestern Development*, Inc. 154 N.W.2d 803 (S.D. 1967).
[37] *See, e.g., Javins* v. *First National Realty Corp.*, 428 F.2d 1021 (D.C. Cir. 1970).

7 LEGAL RULES, PRINCIPLES, AND STANDARDS

The common law consists of three types of norms: legal rules, legal principles, and legal standards. This Chapter considers these three types.

LEGAL RULES

In the common law legal rules are relatively specific legal norms that require actors to act or not act in a specified way, enable or disable specified types of arrangements or dispositions, or set remedies for specified wrongs.

In his article *The Model of Rules*[1] Ronald Dworkin argued for a much different characterization of rules: "My immediate purpose," he said, "is to distinguish principles in the generic sense from rules. . . . The difference between legal principles and legal rules is a logical distinction."[2] It is, he said, that rules have an all-or-nothing character and principles do not.

This is incorrect. To begin with, although rules are relatively specific, they do not operate in an all-or-nothing manner. Strikingly, Dworkin neither defined nor gave an example of a legal rule. He did give an example of a *rule*, but it was not a legal rule; it was a baseball rule. He said, "The all-or-nothing rule is seen most plainly if we look at the way rules operate, *not in law*, but in some enterprise that they dominate—a game, for example. In baseball a rule provides that if the

[1] Ronald Dworkin, *The Model of Rules*, 35 U. CHI. L. REV. 14 (1967).
[2] *Id.* at 23, 25.

batter has had three strikes he is out ... except that the batter who has taken three strikes is not out if the catcher drops the ball."[3]

This is a remarkable passage: To begin with, Dworkin admitted that his all-or-nothing concept of the character of legal rules is not seen most plainly if we look at the way legal rules operate. Instead, he was driven to use a baseball rule to illustrate his argument. The reason that he was driven to use a baseball rule is that legal rules, unlike baseball rules, usually do *not* have an all-or-nothing character. As Fred Schauer writes:

> Ronald Dworkin maintains ... that it is definitional of a rule that it be conclusive if applicable, but this picture appears unfaithful to everyday experience. When I drive in excess of a precise speed limit in order to rush an injured child to the hospital, or when the observant Jew eats pork in order to avoid starvation, the force of the applicable rule has been overridden by more exigent consider-ations. Surely these are rules, if anything is, and just as surely rules are routinely overridden in circumstances comparable to those just mentioned. In these and countless other instances, the reason for action supplied by an applicable rule is not in the particular circum-stances sufficient to resist the reasons for action supplied by other considerations, some of which may but not need be other rules.[4]

Or as Hart and Sacks pointed out: "It is probably a flat impossibility to frame a legal rule applying to any considerable mass of transactions without leaving ... uncertainties."[5]

LEGAL PRINCIPLES

Legal principles are relatively general legal norms. Here too Dworkin advanced a different approach – in fact, two different approaches, both of which are unjustified.

---

[3] *Id.* at 25 (emphasis added). Dworkin's description of the baseball rule is inaccurate. The rule is not that if the batter has taken three strikes he is not out if the catcher drops the ball. Rather, the rule is that a batter who has taken three strikes becomes a base runner if the third strike is not caught by the catcher and either first base is unoccupied or first base is occupied and there are two outs. OFFICIAL BASEBALL RULES 6.09 (2014 ed.).

[4] FREDERICK SCHAUER, PLAYING BY THE RULES 115 (1991).

[5] HENRY M. HART, JR. & ALBERT M. SACKS, THE LEGAL PROCESS 139 (1994) (prepared from the 1958 Tentative Edition by William N. Eskridge, Jr. and Philip P. Frickey).

Under one approach, Dworkin argued that a principle is "a standard that is to be observed, not because it will advance or secure an economic, political, or social situation deemed desirable, but because it is a requirement of justice, fairness, or some other dimension of morality."[6] This is a good definition of a moral principle but it is not a good definition of legal principle. For example, the bargain principle in contract law, under which bargains are normally enforceable according to their terms, is based almost entirely on the ground that it will advance an economic state deemed desirable. So, too, is the principle of contract law that the remedy for breach of a bargain contract is expectation damages, which puts the promisee in the position he would have been in if the contract had been performed. Many other legal principles, including principles of evidence and property law, are also standards to be observed based on the proposition that they will secure an economic or social state deemed desirable.

Under his second approach, Dworkin argued that principles differ logically from rules because rules have an all-or-nothing character and principles do not. But although it is true that principles do not have an all-or-nothing character, neither do rules, so principles cannot be differentiated from rules in this way.

There are differences between legal principles and legal rules, but the proposition that legal rules operate in an all-or-nothing fashion while legal principles don't is not one of these differences. Instead, the differences are:

- Legal rules are relatively specific legal norms while legal principles are relatively general legal norms.
- Because of their generality legal principles can generate, explain, and justify legal rules. In contrast, because of their specificity legal rules cannot generate, explain, or justify either legal principles or other legal rules – with the limited exception that occasionally a new principle may be formulated partly on the ground that it justifies a group of previously free-standing legal rules that had not theretofore been justified by a principle.
- Because legal rules are relatively specific most legal rules can be applied to determine cases with little or no elaboration. In contrast, because legal principles are relatively general many or most legal principles must be elaborated to determine cases. For example, under the legal rule that an

---

[6] Dworkin, *supra* note 1, at 23.

offeree's power to accept an offer is terminated by her rejection of the offer a court can determine, without elaboration of the rule, that an offeree lost her power of acceptance by rejecting an offer. In contrast, a court would usually not be able to determine without elaboration that a contract is unconscionable, because the principle of unconscionability is too general to often justify such a conclusion without further elaboration. Instead, a court will normally resolve an unconscionability case by applying one of the relatively specific rules that the principle of unconscionability has generated, such as the rules that unfair surprise and price-gouging are unconscionable.

LEGAL STANDARDS

As used in legal reasoning, the term *standard* has two different meanings. Sometimes the term is used as a collective noun that includes all legal norms – rules, principles, and standards. This meaning has no substantive significance.

Alternatively, the term is used to refer to legislative rules that are at the outer limits of generality. A subclass of this type of standard is a rule that is not applicable at the moment of its adoption because it is meant to be effective only when elaborated by an administrative agency. Call these deferred standards. Courts, unlike legislatures, very seldom establish rules that are only effective at a later date.

There is a fundamental difference between rules and deferred standards. Rules can be adopted by courts; deferred standards normally cannot be. The reason is that courts normally adopt only rules that apply to the litigants before them and to future actors, and with very limited exceptions do not adopt rules that apply only to future actors.[7]

---

[7] There are a limited number of cases in which a court overrules an established rule and makes the new rule partly or wholly prospective – a technique known as prospective overruling. In the simplest case the new rule is made applicable to the case before the court and transactions or events that occur after the decision in the case but not to transactions or events that occurred before the decision. *See, e.g., Williams* v. *Detroit*, 364 Mich. 231 (1961). In some cases, the new rule is not made applicable even to the case before the court, but only to events or transactions that occur after a designated future date. *See, e.g., Spanel* v. *Mounds View School District* No. 621, 264 Minn. 279 (1962). There are other variations. For an extensive discussion of prospective overruling, *see* MELVIN A. EISENBERG, THE NATURE OF THE COMMON LAW 121–32 (1988).

8 THE MALLEABILITY OF COMMON LAW RULES

Legal rules are either canonical or malleable. A canonical legal rule is fixed: it may not be expressed in different ways, cannot evolve, and cannot be made subject to exceptions. Statutes are the paradigm form of canonical legal rules. In contrast, a malleable rule can be expressed in different ways, can evolve, and can be made subject to exceptions. Common law rules are the paradigm form of malleable legal rules.

The great English legal philosopher H.L.A. Hart famously developed the concept that rules have a core and a penumbra:

> ... A legal rule forbids you to take a vehicle into the public park. Plainly this forbids an automobile, but what about bicycles, roller skates, toy automobiles? What about airplanes? Are these, as we say, to be called "vehicles" for the purpose of the rule or not? If we are to communicate with each other at all, and if, as in the most elementary form of law, we are to express our intentions that a certain type of behavior be regulated by rules, then the general words we use—like "vehicle" in the case I consider—must have some standard instance in which no doubts are felt about its application. There must be a core of settled meaning, but there will be, as well, a penumbra of debatable cases in which words are neither obviously applicable nor obviously ruled out. These cases will each have some features in common with the standard case; they will lack others or be accompanied by features not present in the standard case.[1]

Applying the distinction between core and penumbra, a common law rule can be articulated through more than one expression of the core of

---

[1] H.L.A. Hart, *Positivism and the Separation of Law and Morals*, 71 HARV. L. REV. 593, 607 (1958).

the rule, through evolution of the meaning of the core, through development of exceptions to the core, or through modifications of the rule's penumbra. In each case the core remains, albeit in modified form.

An example of different expressions of the core of a common law rule concerns the rule that damages for breach of contract will be awarded only if they are sufficiently certain. One expression of the core of that rule is that damages based on probability are insufficiently certain. For example, in *Kenford Co.* v. *Erie County*[2] Erie County had made a contract with Dome Stadium, Inc. (DSI) under which Erie would construct a domed stadium, and after the stadium was completed Erie and DSI would negotiate a forty-year lease for its operation by DSI. If a lease could not be agreed on, the parties would execute a twenty-year agreement, in a form appended to the contract, for the management of the stadium by DSI. In the event Erie County did not construct the stadium, thereby breaching the contract. DSI sued for damages, consisting of the profit it would have made under the appended form of agreement, and Erie County defended on the ground that DSI's damages were too uncertain. The New York Court of Appeals held for Erie County notwithstanding the "massive quantity of expert proof submitted by DSI" and the fact that "the procedure for computing damages selected by DSI was in accord with contemporary economic theory and was presented through the testimony of recognized experts," on the ground that DSI's evidence constituted only projections.

Under an alternative expression of the core of the certainty rule damages based on probability can be sufficiently certain. For example, in *Rombola* v. *Cosindas*[3] Rombola agreed to train, maintain, and race Cosindas's horse Margy Sampson during the period November 8, 1962 to December 1, 1963. Rombola was to pay all expenses and receive 75 percent of the gross purses, and Cosindas was to receive the remaining 25 percent. In winter 1962–63 Rombola maintained and trained Margy Sampson at his stable, and the following spring and summer he raced her twenty-five times. In fall 1963 Rombola entered Margy Sampson in six races to be held at a Suffolk Downs meet. Before the meet was held Cosindas took possession of Margy Sampson and

[2] 67 N.E.2d 257 (1986).
[3] 351 Mass. 382 (1966).

thereby deprived Rombola of his right to race her. Rombola sued Cosindas for damages based on the earnings he would have made if he had been allowed to race Margy Sampson for the full contract period. The trial judge directed a verdict for Cosindas on the ground that Rombola's damages were too uncertain. The Massachusetts Supreme Court reversed:

> ... In the year of the contract, of the twenty-five races in which the horse was entered by Rombola, she had won ten and shared in the purse money in a total of twenty races, earning, in all, purses approximating $12,000. In the year following the expiration of Rombola's contract with Cosindas, the horse raced twenty-nine times and won money in an amount almost completely consistent percentagewise with the money won during the period of the contract. ...
>
> We think ... that Rombola would be entitled to show substantial damages on the theory of loss of prospective profits. ... [Margy Sampson] had already proved her ability both prior to and while under Rombola's management and training, over an extended period of time, against many competitors and under varying track conditions. Her consistent performance in the year subsequent to the breach negates any basis for an inference of a diminution in ability or in earning capacity at the time of the Suffolk Downs meet. While it is possible that no profits would have been realized if Margy Sampson had participated in the scheduled stake races, that possibility is inherent in any business venture[4].

Similarly, in *Contemporary Mission, Inc.* v. *Famous Music Corp.*[5] Famous Music breached a contract with Contemporary Mission under which Famous Music agreed to pay royalties to Contemporary Mission in return for the master tape recording of a rock opera, *Virgin*, and the exclusive right to manufacture and sell records made from the master. The contract provided that Famous Music would release at least four singles from *Virgin*. Under the doctrine of *Wood* v. *Lucy*[6] Famous Music had an obligation to promote the singles nationwide. Famous Music breached the contract by prematurely terminating promotion of the singles. Prior to the breach, one of the singles reached Number 80

[4] *Id.* at 384-385.
[5] 357 F.2d 818 (2d Cir. 1977).
[6] 118 N.E. 214 (1917).

on the Hot Soul Singles record charts and after the breach it reached Number 61. At the trial Contemporary Mission offered a statistical analysis of every song that had reached Number 61 during 1974. This analysis showed that 76 percent of the 324 songs that had reached Number 61 ultimately reached the Top 40, 65 percent reached the Top 30, 51 percent reached the Top 20, 34 percent reached the Top 10, 21 percent reached the Top 5, and 10 percent reached Number 1. Contemporary Mission was also prepared to offer the testimony of an expert witness who would have converted these measures of success into projected sales figures and lost royalties. The trial judge excluded this evidence on the ground that it was speculative. The Second Circuit held that the evidence should have been admitted:

> ... This is not a case in which the plaintiff sought to prove hypo-thetical profits from the sale of a hypothetical record at a hypothetical price in a hypothetical market .... [T]he record was real, the price was fixed, the market was buying and the record's success, while modest, was increasing. Even after the promotional efforts ended, [and] the record was withdrawn from the market-place, it was carried, as a result of its own momentum, to an additional 10,000 sales and to a rise from approximately number 80 on the "Hot Soul Singles" chart of Billboard magazine to num-ber 61. It cannot be gainsaid that if someone had continued to promote it, and if it had not been withdrawn from the market, it would have sold more records than it actually did. Thus, it is certain that Contemporary suffered some damage in the form of lost royalties.[7]

The great case of *Hadley* v. *Baxendale*,[8] discussed in Chapter 4, provides an example of the evolution of the core of a rule. That case was decided by the English Exchequer Court in 1854 and the core of the rule it established remains a centerpiece of the law of contracts, although it has significantly evolved over the years.

Recall that in *Hadley* the court held that a party injured by a breach of contract can recover only those damages that either "[1] should reasonably be considered ... as arising naturally, i.e., according to the usual course of things; or [2] may reasonably be supposed to have been

---

[7] *Id.* at 927.
[8] (1854) 156 Eng. Rep. 145, Q. Ex. 341.

in the contemplation of both parties, at the time they made the contract, as the probable result of the breach of it." The two branches of the court's holding have come to be known as the first and second rules of *Hadley* v. *Baxendale*. The first rule collapses into the second because damages that should reasonably be considered as arising naturally from the breach may reasonably be supposed to be in the contemplation of the parties when they made their contract. Damages under the second rule are referred to as consequential damages and are almost always the primary issue in *Hadley* cases. Accordingly, the second rule, which essentially turns on foreseeability, is the core of *Hadley*.

At the outset, the second rule was not infrequently interpreted to exclude consequential damages unless the breaching party had made a tacit agreement to pay such damages. Later, the second rule evolved to preclude consequential damages unless the defendant had reason to know that those damages would be the probable or even highly probable result of the breach. In the modern period, the test for consequential damages under *Hadley* has further evolved. The case law through the 1950s was summarized as follows by Lord Reid in *Koufos* v. *C. Czarnikow, Ltd.*, decided by the House of Lords: "For a considerable time there was a tendency to set narrow limits to awards of damages" under *Hadley*.[9] In *Czarnikow* a shipper had chartered a carrier's vessel to carry a cargo of 300 tons of sugar from Constanza in the Dominican Republic to Basrah in Iraq where the shipper planned to sell the sugar on the open market. A reasonable prediction of the length of the voyage was twenty days but in breach of the contract the carrier had made deviations in the voyage that caused a delay of nine days. The sugar was sold in lots at Basrah between December 12 and 22, but shortly before that time the market price for sugar had fallen, partly due to the arrival of another cargo of sugar.

If not for the delay the sugar would have sold for 32 pounds, 10 shillings per ton, but the actual price realized was 31 pounds, 2 shillings, 9 pence per ton, and the shipper sued the carrier for the difference. The market price of sugar in Basrah could have gone up or down as a result of the late arrival of the shipper's cargo; it was a fifty–fifty chance either way. The court held for the shipper. The five judges

---

[9] 1969 1 App. Cas. 380, 387 (1967).

wrote separate opinions but concurred in the result. Although they differed somewhat on how the second rule of *Hadley* should be expressed, the phrases "liable to result," "real danger," and "serious possibility" met general approval. These phrases, together with the award of damages when it was only a fifty–fifty chance that the market price would go down, constituted a further evolution and liberalization of the core of the *Hadley* rule.

Hector Martinez and Co. v. *Southern Pacific Transp. Co.*[10] involved an even further evolution and liberalization. Martinez had shipped strip-mining machinery by rail via the Southern Pacific railway from Ohio to Eagle Pass, Texas. The machinery was loaded onto five separate railroad cars. Southern Pacific shipped the five cars separately and the last car arrived in Eagle Pass on April 2, 1974. Martinez contended that the last car should have arrived on March 1 and sued Southern Pacific for the fair rental value of the machinery during the period March 1–April 2. The court held for Martinez on the ground that "Capital goods such as machinery have a use value, which may equal the rental value of the equipment or may be an interest value. The latter is ordinarily interest at the market rate on the value of the machine. It might be quite foreseeable that deprivation of the machine's use because of a carriage delay will cause a loss of rental value or interest value during the delay."

Southern Pacific argued that under *Hadley* v. *Baxendale* it should not be held liable because it was as foreseeable that the goods were to be sold as that they were to be used. The Court rejected this argument:

> This contention proves too much because *Hadley* allows recovery for harms that should have been foreseen. The general rule does not require the plaintiff to show that the actual harm suffered was the most foreseeable of possible harms. He need only demonstrate that his harm was not so remote as to make it unforeseeable to a reasonable man at the time of contracting.

A development in *Hadley*'s penumbra involves cases holding that *Hadley* did not apply to the amount of damages, as opposed to the fact of damages. For example, in *Wroth* v. *Tyler*[11] the Court held

[10] 606 F.2d 106 (1979), *cert. denied*, 446 U.S. 982 (1980).
[11] [1974] Ch. 80.

"[that under the second rule of *Hadley* a plaintiff] need only show a contemplation of circumstances which embrace the head or type of damages in question, and need not demonstrate a contemplation of the quantum of damages under that head or type."[12]

The malleability of common law rules was well-expressed by Cardozo: "The rules and principles of case law have never been treated as final truths but as working hypotheses, continually retested in those great laboratories of law, the courts of justice. Every new case is an experiment, and if the accepted rule which seems applicable yields a result which is felt to be unjust, the rule is reconsidered."[13]

Fred Schauer argues that because common law rules are malleable they are not rules:

> [T]he absence of continuous malleability is ... a necessary ... condition for rule-based decision making. ...[14]
>
> [T]he issue ... is whether rules may be subject to exceptions added at the moment of application ... and still be rules, and the answer to that question is "no."[15]
>
> If what appears to be a rule can thus be modified when its indications are inconsistent with the wise policy or the purpose behind the rule ... then it appears that common law "rules" are ... descriptive rather than prescriptive ....[16]

This argument is incorrect: all common law rules are malleable and all common law rules are rules. The core of all common law rules can be expressed in different ways, and can evolve, even while they remain rules. The penumbra of all common law rules can be augmented or otherwise changed even while the core remains a rule.

---

[12] Accord: *Brown* v. *KMR Services Ltd.* [1995] All E.R. 598 (1995). Contra: Victoria Laundry [Windsor] Ltd., 1949 2 K.B. 528.

[13] Benjamin Cardozo, The Nature of the Judicial Process 23 (1921).

[14] Frederick Schauer, Playing by the Rules 84 (1993).

[15] *Id.* at 116.

[16] *Id.* at 177.

9 HIVING OFF NEW LEGAL RULES FROM ESTABLISHED LEGAL RULES, CREATING EXCEPTIONS TO ESTABLISHED RULES, AND DISTINGUISHING

It is often said that a court faced with a binding precedent that on its face governs the case before it must either apply or distinguish the precedent. This characterization of a deciding court's choice is too narrow. More accurately, a court faced with a binding precedent that on its face governs the case before it must either apply the precedent, hive off a new rule from the rule established by the precedent, create an exception to the rule, distinguish the precedent, or overrule it. This Chapter concerns the last three of these modes of legal reasoning.

HIVING OFF A NEW LEGAL RULE FROM A RULE ESTABLISHED IN A BINDING PRECEDENT

In hiving off, a new legal rule is carved out of a rule established in a binding precedent, to govern an issue that prior to the hiving off fell within the established rule. The new rule then lives side-by-side with the established rule, just as a swarm of bees hives off to create a new colony while the old colony remains in place. Typically the reason for hiving off is that although the established rule was generally desirable it had become apparent that it was undesirable to apply the rule to a subclass of cases to which the rule would otherwise apply. The court therefore hives off a new rule to cover the subclass.

For example, until the early part of the twentieth century it was an established rule that, with very limited exceptions, simple donative promises – promises to make a gift – were normally unenforceable. There were good reasons for this rule.

For one thing, unlike bargain promises, which are usually supported by objective evidence, simple donative promises are often made out of the blue, with no evidentiary context, no writing, and no witnesses. As a result, it would be too easy to fabricate a simple donative promise and falsely convince a jury that such a promise was made.

Next, again unlike bargain promises, simple donative promises are typically made in an affective context and often made in a surge of transient emotion, and therefore without deliberation.

Then too, making simple donative promises enforceable would tend to decrease the value of such promises. An enforceability regime would commodify and therefore impoverish, simple donative promises because it would never be clear to either the promisor or the promisee whether a donative promise that was *made* in a spirit of love, friendship, affection, or the like was *performed* for those reasons or instead was performed to discharge a legal obligation or avoid a lawsuit.

Under this rule it did not matter that the promisee had relied upon the promise. However, beginning in 1932, under the impetus of the Restatement of Contracts the courts hived off a new rule, known as the principle of promissory estoppel, under which a donative promise was enforceable if it was foreseeably relied upon by the promisee. In creating this rule the courts narrowed but did not abandon the established rule concerning donative promises. Instead, the courts held that although simple donative promises were normally unenforceable a hived-off new rule should be created to deal with foreseeably relied-upon donative promises. Effectively the courts concluded that the established rule was desirable only if the donative promisee suffered no loss as a result of the promisor's breaking its loss promise. However, where a donative promisee foreseeably suffered a as a result of the promisor's breach, as a matter of social morality the promisor should compensate the promisee for that loss.

To put it differently, when it was foreseeable that breaking a donative promise would cause a loss to the promisee, the importance of compensating the promisee for its loss outweighed the reasons supporting the established rule in the absence of such a loss.

CREATING EXCEPTIONS

Another alternative to applying a rule established in a binding precedent is to create an exception to the rule, thereby limiting its ambit. Exceptions differ in a fundamental way from rules that are hived off. Rules that are hived off are free-standing – that is, once hived off from an established rule the hived-off rule lives independently. In contrast, exceptions are parasitical on an established rule, in the sense that they have no meaning except in the context of the rule from which they are exceptions. Thus, one way to understand exceptions is as unless clauses – if there is an exception X to established rule ABC that rule has been effectively reformulated to be ABC unless X.

Exceptions fall into two categories: those that are consistent with the rule and those that are not. The term *inconsistent* is ambiguous. Under one interpretation of the term, two propositions are inconsistent if and only if one meaning negates or contradicts the other.[1] Under an alternative interpretation two propositions are inconsistent if they are not reasonably harmonious.[2] I adopt the former interpretation.

Consistent Exceptions

Many or most exceptions are consistent with the rule to which they are exceptions. This is exemplified by some exceptions in the law of contracts and the law of evidence.

Contract Law
Under contract law promises that are enforceable are said to have consideration, and under the bargain principle bargain promises have consideration. A bargain is an exchange in which each party views what it agrees to do as the price of what the other party agrees to do. The

[1] *Cf. Hunt Foods and Industries* v. *Doliner,* 26 A.D.2d 41 (1966).
[2] *Cf.* Alaska Northern Development, *Inc.* v. *Alyeska Pipeline Service Co.,* 666 P.2d 33 (Alaska 1983), *cert. denied,* 464 U.S. 1041 (1984).

enforceability of bargain promises is based on strong social policies. For one thing, bargains create gains through trade, because normally each party values what it will get more highly than what it will give. For another, free-enterprise societies depend heavily on private planning, and bargains facilitate such planning.

There are many exceptions to the bargain principle, most of which are consistent with the principle. For example, a bargain is not enforceable against a minor, or a person who by reason of mental illness or defect was unable to understand the nature and consequences of the bargain, or where the promisee had reason to know that the promisor was intoxicated and that as a result was unable to understand the nature and consequences of the transaction or to act in a reasonable manner in relation to the transaction.[3] These exceptions are consistent with the bargain principle because that principle is based on the premise that contracting parties who have full capacity are the best judges of their own utility, and the exceptions concern cases where a party does not or is unlikely to have full capacity.

Evidence Law

Traditionally the law of evidence was judicially made. However, in 1975 Congress adopted the Federal Rules of Evidence, which codified the law of evidence. The Federal Rules of Evidence apply only to federal courts, but most states have adopted a counterpart of those Rules.[4] Although this book concerns reasoning in the common law and the law of evidence is now codified, because the codification is largely based on the common law I will employ the Federal Rules to further exemplify consistent exceptions.

A fundamental rule of evidence is the hearsay rule. Hearsay is a statement made by a person, known as a declarant, who does not make the statement while testifying at the trial in which the declarant's statement is sought to be introduced, and which a party to the trial offers in evidence to prove a claim.[5] Under the hearsay rule such a statement is inadmissible unless it falls within an exception to the

---

[3] See RESTATEMENT OF CONTRACTS. sections 14–16.

[4] GRAHAM C. LILLY, DANIEL J. CAPRA & STEPHEN A. SALTZBURG, PRINCIPLES OF THE LAW OF EVIDENCE 151 (8th ed. 2019).

[5] See FEDERAL RULES OF EVIDENCE Rule 801(c).

rule. The reason for the hearsay rule is stated as follows in Lilly, Capra, and Saltzberg, *Principles of the Law of Evidence*:

> The rule against hearsay is designed to exclude statements that are not reliable when offered to prove that what a person said was true. The classic hearsay situation is this: a witness testifies that someone else [the declarant] made a statement about an event that is in dispute at the trial. The witness relates the statement, but cannot verify that the declarant was telling the truth. If the statement is offered to prove [that] what the declarant said was true, then there is no way to verify for accuracy. The declarant is not at trial. He is not speaking under oath. The factfinder does not get to view him and make its own assessment of whether he is speaking the truth. Most importantly, he is not subject to the crucible of cross-examination.[6]

Under the Federal Rules of Evidence there are twenty-nine exceptions to the hearsay rule and four exemptions that are exceptions for all practical purposes. I will focus on the exceptions embodied in Rules 803(3) and (4).

Rule 803(3) makes an exception to the hearsay rule for statements of the declarant's state of mind, such as the declarant's motive, intent, or plan, or statements of the declarant's emotional, sensory, or physical condition, such as mental feeling, pain, or bodily health. The rationale for this exception is that when a declarant is speaking about its existing state of mind the dangers of mistaken perception and faulty memory are minimized.[7]

Rule 803(4) makes an exception to the hearsay rule for statements that are made for and are reasonably pertinent to medical diagnosis or treatment and describe medical history, past or present symptoms or sensations, their inception, or their general cause. The reason for this exception is that normally a declarant has every incentive to be truthful when making such a statement.

The exceptions to the hearsay rule in Rules 803(3) and (4) are consistent with the hearsay rule because the purpose of that rule is to exclude unreliable testimony and the exceptions concern statements that are highly likely to be reliable.

---

[6] LILLY ET AL., *supra* note 4, at 151.
[7] *Id.* at 212.

Inconsistent Exceptions

Some exceptions to established rules are inconsistent with the rules. An example is the preexisting duty rule in contract law and the exceptions to the rule. Under that rule if A and B, who are parties to a bargain, make a new bargain to modify their contract, in which A promises to do only what he had a preexisting legal duty to do in exchange for B's promise to pay more than she agreed to pay under the original contract, the modification is said to lack consideration and is unenforceable.

The preexisting duty rule is both inconsistent with the bargain principle and unsound, because modifications are bargains and the reasons for enforcing bargains are fully applicable to modifications since there are usually good reasons for modifications. Many or most modifications are motivated by the fact that when the time comes for A to perform the world looks significantly different than A and B expected it to look when they made their contract, and B agrees that as a matter of fair dealing it is appropriate to modify the contract to reflect the purpose of the contract or the equities as they now stand. Another, reason for modifications is reciprocity or the hope of reciprocity. A modification that appears to be one-sided if examined in isolation may be reciprocal when account is taken of the dynamic ebb and flow of the contractual stream in which the modification is located. For example, B may agree to a modification that favors A to reciprocate for past modifications that favored B. Or B may believe that her agreement to a modification will increase the possibility that A will agree to a modification in B's favor when B is in A's shoes.

Not only is the preexisting duty rule inconsistent with the bargain principle: the courts have made exceptions to the preexisting duty rule that are inconsistent with the rule. The reason for this is simple. An inconsistent exception to an unsound rule yields a sound result.

Under one exception the preexising duty rule is inapplicable if the preexisting duty was owed to a third person.[8] This exception is inconsistent with the rule because under the rule a promise to perform an act that the promisor is under a preexisting duty to perform is *not*

---

[8] *See, e.g., Morrison Flying Service* v. *Deming Nat'l Bank,* 404 F.2d 856 (10th Cir. 1968).

consideration, and under this exception a promise to perform an act that the promisor is under a preexisting duty to perform *is* consideration.

Under another exception the preexisting duty rule is inapplicable to a modification consisting of payment of part of an unliquidated debt (that is, a debt whose amount is not fixed) that is admittedly due in exchange for the creditor's surrender of its right to collect the balance of the debt.[9] This exception is inconsistent with the preexisting duty rule because the debtor was under a preexisting duty to pay the part of the debt.

Under still another, extremely important exception, adopted in Restatement of Contracts section 89 and *Angel* v. *Murray*,[10] the pre-existing duty rule is inapplicable if the modification is fair and equitable in light of circumstances not anticipated when the contract was made. This exception is inconsistent with the preexisting duty rule because whether a bargain has consideration does not depend on whether the bargain is fair and equitable but only on the fact that a bargain was made. Furthermore, this exception almost blows up the rule because it is likely that most modifications are agreed to because they are fair and equitable. This is evidenced by the results of a questionnaire that Russel Weintraub sent to the general counsels of 182 corporations, forty-five percent of whom responded.[11] One question was "If, because of a shift in market prices, one of your suppliers or customers requested a modification of the contract price, would your company always insist on compliance with the contract?" Ninety-five percent of the respondents replied that their companies would not always insist on compliance. A follow-up question asked the respondents what factors they took into consideration in deciding whether to grant a request for a modification. Eighty percent of the respondents said they would take into account whether relations with the company that made the request had been long and satisfactory, and seventy-six percent said they would take into account whether the request was reasonable under trade practice. In most cases, the respondents reported, the request for

---

[9] *See, e.g., Cohen* v. *Sabin*, 307 A.2d 846 (Pa. 1973).
[10] 322 A.2d 630 (R.I. 1974).
[11] Russell J. Weintraub, *A Survey of Contract Practice and Policy*, 1992 Wis. L. Rev. 1 (1992).

a modification was amicably worked out either by a modification of the contract or by adjustments in future contracts.

So courts sometimes make inconsistent exceptions to established rules. But since consistency in legal reasoning is a value, why do courts adopt inconsistent exceptions rather than simply overrule the established rule?

To begin with, a court may believe that it is important for the judiciary to preserve the appearance of doctrinal stability, and that this appearance would be undermined by frequent overruling. Making inconsistent exceptions helps to resolve that tension because an inconsistent exception to an unsound rule yields a good result while preserving the appearance of doctrinal stability, since it does not involve overruling. Or a court may not be highly confident that the established rule is unsound and may give effect to its uncertainty by creating an inconsistent exception as a provisional step toward full overruling. This approach allows the issue whether the established rule should be overruled to percolate so that it can be considered in the professional discourse, consisting of decisions by other courts and scholarly commentary.

Next, making inconsistent exceptions may be used as a technique for dealing with the problem of reliance on precedents. Making an inconsistent exception allows a court to protect those who relied on the core of an established rule while signaling to the profession that the rule is a candidate for full overruling and therefore is not reliable.

DISTINGUISHING

Instead of applying a precedent that appears or plausibly appears to apply to a case before it a court may conclude that the precedent is distinguishable. Distinguishing is often regarded as a unified process, but in fact there are three types of distinguishing: fact-based distinguishing, rule-based distinguishing, and socially based distinguishing.

In fact-based distinguishing a court concludes that a precedent should not be applied to the case before it because of a difference between the facts of the two cases. In one form of fact-based distinguishing a significant fact of the precedent does not have a counterpart in the case to be decided. For example, suppose that a precedent held that an offeree's rejection of an offer terminates the offeree's power of acceptance and that facts A, B, and C showed that the offeree rejected the offer. In the case to be decided there is no counterpart to fact C The deciding court then explicitly or implicitly reaffirms the rule that an offeree's rejection terminates the offeree's power of acceptance but distinguishes the precedent because due to the absence of a counterpart to fact C it cannot be concluded that the offeree in the case before it rejected the offer. In a second form a significant fact in the case to be decided does not have a counterpart in the precedent. For example, suppose that in the precedent the facts were A, B, and C, and in the case to be decided the facts are A, B, C, and D. The deciding court then explicitly or implicitly affirms the rule that a rejection terminates the offeree's power of acceptance but distinguishes the case to be decided on the ground that fact D showed that the offeree in the case before it had not rejected the offer.

In rule-based distinguishing the deciding court holds that a precedent that plausibly applies to the case before the court does not do so in fact. For example, in *Mathis* v. *Hoffman*[12] plaintiffs and defendant owned two adjoining parcels of land. In 2004 plaintiffs constructed a fence between the two parcels at a cost of more than $15,000. In 2008, a survey showed that the fence was on the defendant's land. Plaintiffs offered to relocate the fence onto their property at no cost to defendant, but she refused to allow plaintiffs to remove the fence. Plaintiffs then sought an injunction granting them the right to remove the fence and relocate the fence onto their property. The trial court granted the injunction. On appeal, defendant contended that she was entitled to a choice of either allowing plaintiffs to remove the fence or being made subject to a claim of unjust enrichment, relying on *Beacon Homes, Inc.* v. *Holt.*[13] In that case the plaintiff, without the defendant's permission, had constructed a house on land owned by the defendant in the good faith but mistaken belief that the land was owned by a third party who had contracted with the plaintiff to have the house built. The plaintiff sought to remove the house, the defendant

---

[12] 711 S.E. 2d 825 (N.C. Ct. App. 2011).
[13] 266 N.C. 467 (1966).

refused, and the plaintiff brought an action for unjust enrichment. The defendant demurred. The court overruled the demurrer on the ground that the complaint stated a good cause of action for unjust enrichment. The court distinguished *Beacon Homes* on the ground that it did not hold that a defendant property owner must be allowed to choose what remedy it prefers to offer a plaintiff who has mistakenly constructed an improvement on the defendant's property.

In socially based distinguishing an exception is drawn to a precedent either because the social propositions that supported the precedent do not extend to the case before the court or because the case before the court involves social propositions that were not applicable to the precedent. For example, suppose a precedent held that bargains are enforceable. Now the question comes before a court, is a bargain made by a minor enforceable against the minor. The court distinguishes the precedent on the ground that a reason for the principle that the precedent established was that generally speaking actors are the best judges of their own utility, or preference, and minors are not.

Distinguishing differs in two respects from hiving off and the creation of exceptions.

First, in hiving off and creating exceptions the deciding court either establishes a new rule or modifies an established rule. In theory, drawing a distinction might also establish a new rule or modify an existing rule but in practice it seldom does so, because most distinctions are one-offs based on an individualized difference between the facts of the precedent and those of the case before the court and are not easily generalizable. Distinguishing usually requires neither the creation of a new rule nor the modification of an existing rule. On the contrary, distinguishing courts normally explicitly or implicitly reaffirm the established rule.

Second, a lower court normally cannot hive off a new rule from a rule established by a superior court and thereby limit the scope of that rule. Similarly, a lower court normally cannot create an exception to a rule established by a superior court. However, a lower court can distinguish a rule established by a superior court.[14]

---

[14] *See* JOSEPH RAZ, THE AUTHORITY OF LAW 186 (1979).

Joseph Raz argues that distinguishing a rule means modifying the rule and requires that the modified rule must be the established rule restricted by the addition of a further condition for its application.[15] This is incorrect. To begin with a distinguishing court almost never modifies the rule it distinguishes. Instead, a distinguishing court normally explicitly or implicitly *reaffirms* the rule established in the precedent but distinguishes it on the ground that the precedent is inapplicable, not that the precedent should be modified.

Larry Alexander and Emily Sherman argue that "distinguishing precedent cases just *is* overruling them."[16] This, too, is incorrect. A distinguishing court normally does not overrule the precedent. On the contrary, normally a distinguishing court explicitly or implicitly reaffirms the precedent but concludes that the precedent does not apply to the case before it.

In principle, the manner in which courts make exceptions and the manner in which courts draw distinctions is highly comparable. In practice, there is a critical difference between the two modes. When a court a court makes an exception the exception becomes part of the rule. When a court draws a distinction the distinction is likely to apply only to that case.

[15] *Id.*
[16] LARRY ALEXANDER & EMILY SHERMAN, DEMYSTIFYING LEGAL REASONING 124 (2008) (emphasis in original).

10 ANALOGY-BASED LEGAL REASONING

This Chapter concerns analogy-based legal reasoning in the common law. In most fields in which reasoning by analogy plays a role, such as science, reasoning by analogy is based on similarity. Similarity-based analogical reasoning generally takes the following form:

A, an object, entity, or scenario (often referred to as the source) has the characteristics a, b, c, d, and e.

B, an object, entity, or scenario (often referred to as the target) has the characteristics a, b, c, and d.

Because A and B are highly similar it is fair to infer that B is just like A in all respects and therefore also has the characteristic e.

Some commentators claim that reasoning by analogy in law is also based on similarity. For example, Lloyd Weinreb wrote, "[S]imilarity [is] at the heart of an analogical argument."[1] Grant Lamond writes, "An analogical argument in legal reasoning is an argument that a case should be treated in a certain way because that is the way a similar case has been treated."[2] And Emily Sherwin writes, "The analogical method, as commonly practiced, works something like this: confronted with an unsettled question, the judge surveys past decisions, identifies ways in which these decisions are similar to or different from each other and the question before her, and develops a principle that captures the similarities and differences she considers important."[3] These claims

---

[1] LLOYD WEINREB, LEGAL REASON: THE USE OF ANALOGY IN LEGAL ARGUMENT 5 (2d ed. 2016).

[2] Grant Lamond, *Precedent and Analogy in Legal Reasoning, in* THE STANFORD ENCYCLOPEDIA OF PHILOSOPHY (2006).

[3] Emily Sherwin, *A Defense of Analogical Reasoning in Law*, 66 U. CHI. L. REV. 1179, 1179 (1999).

are incorrect because law is based not on characteristics but on rules. Accordingly, although reasoning by analogy in the common law is occasionally based on similarity it is more fundamentally and much more often based on rules.

In rule-based analogy reasoning a court begins with an established legal rule—call it the given rule—that is not literally applicable to the case to be decided, and extends the rule to cover that case because as a matter of social propositions the given rule and the case to be decided cannot be meaningfully distinguished.

For example, in *Adams* v. *New Jersey Steamship Company*.[4] Adams was a passenger in a stateroom on a steamboat owned by the New Jersey Steamboat Company (the Company). When Adams retired to his stateroom for the evening he locked up, but a thief nevertheless stole his money, apparently by reaching through a window. The Company was not negligent in regard to the theft, but Adams sued for his loss on the ground that the Company was liable as an insurer – that is, strictly liable for the loss without proof of negligence.

For the purpose of analogical reasoning the Court had not one but three possible analogical rules from among which to choose. One analogy was the rule that innkeepers were liable as insurers where property was stolen from a guest's room. A second analogy was the rule that common carriers were liable as insurers for the personal baggage of passengers. A third analogy was the rule that railroads were not liable as insurers for money taken from passengers while they were in their berths in sleeping cars. The court selected the first analogy on the ground that the public policy that made innkeepers liable as insurers for thefts from guestrooms should be extended by analogy to make steamship companies liable for thefts from staterooms:

> The principle on which innkeepers are charged by the common law as insurers of the money or personal effects of their guests origin-ated in public policy. It was deemed to be a sound and necessary rule that [innkeepers] should be subjected to a high degree of responsibility in cases where an extraordinary confidence is neces-sarily reposed in them, and where ... danger of plunder exists by reason of the peculiar relations of the parties .... The relations that

[4] 151 N.Y. 163 (1896).

exist between a steamboat company and its passengers, who have procured a stateroom for their comfort during the journey, differ in no essential respect from those that exist between the innkeeper and his guests.

... No good reason is apparent for relaxing the rigid rule of the common law which applies as between innkeeper and guest, since the same considerations of public policy apply to both relations.

Similarly, in *Oppenheimer* v. *Kreidel*[5] a wife sued her husband's paramour, Kreidel, for criminal conversation. This is a tort, now widely abrogated by statute, that traditionally gave a husband whose wife had committed adultery a right to sue her paramour. Kreidel moved to dismiss the wife's suit on the ground that only a husband could bring such a suit. The New York Court rejected this defense and held that a wife could bring such an action by analogy to the husband's right:

[W]hatever reasons there were for giving the husband at common law the right to maintain an action for adultery committed with his wife, exist to-day in behalf of the woman for a like illegal act committed with her husband. If he had feelings and honor which were hurt by such improper conduct, who will say to-day that she has not the same, perhaps even a keener sense, of the wrong done to her and to the home? If he considered it a defilement of the marriage-bed, why should not she view it in the same light? The statements that he had a property interest in her body and a right to the personal enjoyment of his wife are archaic unless used in a refined sense worthy of the times and which give to the wife the same interest in her husband. ... The danger of doubt being thrown upon the legitimacy of the children, which seems to be the principal reason assigned in all the authorities for the protection of the husband and the maintenance of the action by him, may be offset by the interest which the wife has in the bodily and mental health of her children when they are legitimate. ... So far as I can see there is no sound and legitimate reason for denying a cause of action for criminal conversation to the wife while giving it to the husband. Surely she is as much interested as the husband in maintaining the home and wholesome, clean and affectionate relationships. Her feelings must be as sensitive as his toward the

---

[5] 236 N.Y. 156, 140 N.E. 227 (1928).

intruder, and it would be mere willful blindness on the part of the courts to ignore these facts.[6]

Three leading legal scholars, Ronald Dworkin, Richard Posner, and Larry Alexander, claim that reasoning by analogy is invalid. For Dworkin, "An analogy is a way of stating a conclusion, not a way of reaching one."[7] For Posner, "Reasoning by analogy as a mode of judicial expression is a surface phenomenon. It belongs not to legal thought, but to legal rhetoric."[8] For Alexander, analogical reasoning in the law "is a chimera."[9] These claims are also inaccurate. As illustrated in *Adams* and *Oppenheimer*, rule-based analogical reasoning is a valid mode of legal reasoning.

However, although this mode of legal reasoning is valid, it is infrequently employed and therefore is unimportant as a practical matter, because no court would reason by analogy where a legal rule governs the case and the common law is rich with legal rules. Moreover, analogy-based legal reasoning is an extremely weak form of legal reasoning as compared to rule-based legal reasoning because a rule established in a binding precedent normally controls a case to be decided while courts are free to reject an analogy, and even where a court does reason by analogy, it may have several analogies from among which to choose, as was the case in *Adams* v. *New Jersey Steamboat Company*.

---

[6] 236 N.Y. at 160.
[7] Ronald Dworkin, *In Praise of Theory*, 25 ARIZ. L. REV. 353, 371 (1997).
[8] Richard Posner, *Reasoning by Analogy*, 91 CORNELL L. REV. 761, 765 (2006).
[9] Larry Alexander, *The Banality of Legal Reasoning*, 73 NOTRE DAME L. REV. 517, 533 (1998).

11 THE ROLES OF LOGIC, DEDUCTION, AND GOOD JUDGMENT IN LEGAL REASONING

This Chapter concerns the roles of logic, deduction, and good judgment in legal reasoning.

LOGIC

There are many schools of formal logic – the entry on logic in the *Encyclopedia of Philosophy* is almost sixty pages long. In everyday speech, however, the term *logic* is used informally to mean sound reasoning, rather than reasoning that satisfies the criteria of formal logic. So if A and B are engaged in an argument and A says to B "Your argument is not logical," what A normally means is that "Your reasoning is unsound," as in "Your argument is internally inconsistent" or "Your argument doesn't make sense." In law, logic has the same meaning. So when we say that a judicial opinion is logical we mean not that it conforms to the rules of formal logic but that its reasoning is sound.

DEDUCTION

Deduction is a reasoning process in which a conclusion necessarily follows from stated premises. Deduction normally takes the form of a syllogism. A syllogism consists of a general statement, known as the major premise; a specific statement, known as the minor premise; and a conclusion that necessarily follows from the two premises. Here is a famous example:

Major premise: All men are mortal.
Minor premise: Socrates is a man.
Conclusion: Socrates is mortal.

It is sometimes thought that deduction is an important form of legal reasoning. It isn't. As A.G. Guest observed, "only very occasionally have judges cast their reasoning in syllogistic form."[1] There are several reasons why this is so. To begin with, although most or all common law cases involve implicit informal deductive reasoning – as in "It is a rule that the rejection of an offer terminates an offeree's power of acceptance; the offeree rejected the offer; therefore the offeree's power of acceptance was terminated" – few common law cases involve explicit formal deduction. This is partly because the law is concerned with truth but formal deduction is not. There is a difference between whether a syllogism is valid and whether it is sound. A syllogism is valid if its conclusion necessarily follows from its premises, even if its premises are untrue. A syllogism is sound only if its premises are true. Here is an example of a valid but unsound syllogism:

All movie stars have six fingers on their right hand.
Tom Hanks is a movie star.
Therefore Tom Hanks has six fingers on his right hand.

There is another reason why syllogistic deduction is not important in legal reasoning. A judicial opinion normally consists of three elements: a statement of the facts, a statement of the legal rule that governs the case, and an application of the rule to the facts. None of these elements can properly be determined through deduction.

First, the facts of a case normally are determined through testimony, not through deduction.

Next, the application of a rule to the facts of a case can seldom, if ever, be a matter of deduction. As H.L.A. Hart pointed out, rules normally have a core and a penumbra, and the application of

---

[1] A.G. Guest, *Logic in the Law, in* OXFORD ESSAYS IN JURISPRUDENCE 176, 194 (1991).

a penumbra of a rule to the facts of a case cannot be accomplished by formal deduction because penumbral rules are uncertain:

> There must be a core of settled meaning [of a rule], but there will be, as well, a penumbra of debatable cases in which words are neither obviously applicable nor obviously ruled out. . . .
>
> We may call the problems which arise outside the hard core of standard instances or settled meaning "problems of the penumbra"; they are always with us . . . . If a penumbra of uncertainty must surround all legal rules, then their application to specific cases in the penumbra cannot be a matter of logical deduction, and so deductive reasoning, which for generations has been cherished as the very perfection of human reasoning, cannot serve as a model for what judges . . . should do in bringing particular cases under general rules.[2]

Even the core of a common-law rule often cannot be stated with the certainty needed for a syllogism to be sound. To begin with, a rule may have become incongruent with social morality, social policy, and experience and therefore uncertain because it is subject to overruling. Next, a rule is always subject to as-yet-unarticulated exceptions. For example, suppose that, at a certain point in time there is an unqualified rule that bargain promises are enforceable. A case now arises, for the first time, in which a party to a bargain is a minor and the adult party seeks to enforce the bargain against the minor. If the rule that bargain promises are enforceable could be conclusively stated as the major premise of a syllogism the minor would be liable. The major premise would be that bargains are enforceable. The minor premise would be that the minor had made a bargain. The conclusion would be that the minor was liable. But this syllogism is invalid because it does not include an exception that a court would almost certainly draw, namely, that a bargain is not enforceable against a minor.

Finally, legal rules are not based on deduction; they are rules that were established in binding legal precedents, rules that are set out in authoritative although not legally binding sources, and rules that are adopted on the basis of social morality, social policy, and experience.

---

[2] H.L.A. Hart, *The Separation of Law and Morals*, 71 HARV. L. REV. 593, 607–08 (1958).

GOOD JUDGMENT

Good judgment is an important element of legal reasoning – much more so than logic or deduction. Good judgment is easier to recognize than to define, but essentially in legal reasoning it consists of the ability to make sound and well-rooted decisions based on precedent and principle together with a breadth of vision and an understanding of how law can advance the common good.

The role of good judgment in legal reasoning is pervasive. For example, good judgment is needed to apply the penumbra of a rule to a given case, to understand when a rule should be distinguished and when exceptions to a rule should be made, to establish new rules where a case is not governed by an existing rule, and to establish transitions in the law – for example, Cardozo's adoption of a transition from a regime in which manufacturers were generally not liable for injuries caused by their negligence to a regime in which manufacturers are as liable for their negligence as are all other persons (see Chapter 15); Wiley Rutledge's adoption of a transition from a regime in which charitable institutions were normally not liable for injuries caused by their negligence to a regime in which they were; or the Florida Supreme Court's transition from a regime in which there was no right of privacy to a regime in which the right of privacy was a centerpiece of private law.

The importance of good judgment as an element of legal reasoning is frequently overlooked, perhaps because the faculty of good judgment cannot be taught and is hard to acquire. It is a quality, like grace or a discerning eye, that some have and some don't. It differs from intelligence; a person can be very intelligent but still not have good judgment. Good judges have good judgment. Great judges have excellent judgment. It is the quality that makes them great.

12 REASONING FROM HYPOTHETICALS

This Chapter concerns reasoning from hypotheticals. The term *hypothetical* means a fact that is assumed rather than actual. The term *a hypothetical* means a scenario composed of such facts.

Reasoning from hypotheticals is employed throughout the legal process—in adjudication, in oral arguments, and in law school teaching. In adjudication reasoning from hypotheticals take two forms.

In one form a court employs a hypothetical to view the case before it in a broader perspective to help decide the case. Hypotheticals in this form have three characteristics: (1) the hypothetical differs from the case in its particulars, but as a matter of social morality, social policy, and experience the hypothetical is comparable to the case in its basic structure. (2) Intuitively, the hypothetical is easier to decide than the case. (3) Because the basic structure of the hypothetical and the case are comparable as a matter of social propositions, the hypothetical and the case cannot be justifiably distinguished. That being so, the result in the case should be the same as the result in the hypothetical.

For example, in *Vincent* v. *Lake Erie Transportation Co.*[1] Lake Erie's vessel *The Reynolds* was moored to Vincent's dock for the purpose of unloading her cargo. In the course of unloading a violent storm arose, which caused navigation to be suspended for two days. During this period the persons in charge of the vessel kept her lines fast to the dock, and as soon as a line parted or chafed it was replaced. The storm's wind and waves struck *The Reynolds* with such force that it was continually thrown into and damaging the dock. Vincent sued Erie for

---

[1] 109 Minn. 456 (1910).

90

the damage and recovered a verdict of $500 (much higher in today's dollars). On appeal, Erie argued that it was not liable by virtue of the doctrine of necessity, under which a person can use another's property without permission if the use is necessary to prevent injury or loss of life. The court held for Vincent, reasoning in part on the basis of a hypothetical:

> The situation was one in which the ordinary rules regulating property rights were suspended by forces beyond human control, and if, without the direct intervention of some act by the one sought to be held liable, the property of another was injured, such injury must be attributed to the act of God, and not to the wrongful act of the person sought to be charged. ... [H]ere those in charge of the vessel deliberately and by their direct efforts held her in such a position that the damage to the dock resulted, and, having thus preserved the ship at the expense of the dock, it seems to us that her owners are responsible to the dock owners to the extent of the injury inflicted. ...
>
> Theologians hold that a starving man may, without moral guilt, take what is necessary to sustain life; but it could hardly be said that the obligation would not be upon such person to pay the value of the property so taken when he became able to do so. And so public necessity, in times of war or peace, may require the taking of private property for public purposes; but under our system of jurisprudence compensation must be made.
>
> Let us imagine in this case that for the better mooring of the vessel those in charge of her had appropriated a valuable cable lying upon the dock. No matter how justifiable such appropriation might have been, it would not be claimed that, because of the overwhelming necessity of the situation, the owner of the cable could not recover its value. ...
>
> This is ... a case ... where the defendant prudently and advisedly availed itself of the plaintiffs' property for the purpose of preserving its own more valuable property, and the plaintiffs are entitled to compensation for the injury done.

The court's use of its hypothetical illustrates reasoning from a hypothetical to view a case in a broader perspective. The question in the *case* was whether compensation should be paid for having taken an action that was necessary to prevent a decrease in one's own wealth in the face of catastrophic circumstances but that incidentally decreased another's wealth. The question in the *hypothetical* was whether compensation should be paid for having appropriated another person's property when it was necessary to do so to maintain one's own wealth in the face of catastrophic circumstances. The latter case makes a somewhat stronger intuitive case for compensation than the former. However, as a matter of social propositions, it is hard to see why compensation should be due in one case but not the other.

Day v. *Caton*[2] is another case involving reasoning by hypothetical to allow the court to view the case before it in a broader perspective. Day and Caton owned adjoining lots, and Day built a brick party wall that straddled the line between the lots. Because half the wall was on Caton's lot Caton could use it as the fourth wall of a building on his lot. Day therefore asked Caton to pay half the value of the wall. Caton declined, and Day brought suit. The trial court ruled that Caton would be liable if Day built the wall with the expectation that Caton would pay for half its value and Caton knew that Day had that expectation and stood silently by while Day built the wall. The jury returned a verdict for Day, and Caton appealed on the ground that the trial court's ruling was incorrect. The Massachusetts Supreme Court held for Day, reasoning in part on the basis of a hypothetical:

> If a person saw day after day a laborer at work in his field doing services, which must of necessity ensure to his benefit, knowing that the laborer expected pay for his work, when it was perfectly easy to notify him if his services were not wanted, even if a request were not expressly proved, such a request, either previous to or contemporaneous with the performance of the services, might fairly be inferred. But if the fact was merely brought to his attention upon a single occasion and casually, if he had little opportunity to notify the other that he did not desire the work and should not pay for it, or could only do so at the expense of much time and trouble, the same inference might not be made. The circumstances of each case would necessarily determine whether silence with a knowledge that another was doing valuable work for his benefit, and with the expectation of payment, indicated that consent which would give rise to the inference of a contract. The question would be one for

---

[2] 119 Mass. 513 (1876).

the jury, and to them it was properly submitted in the case before us by the presiding judge.[3]

Like *Vincent* v. *Lake Erie*, *Day* v. *Caton* illustrates reasoning by hypothetical to allow a court to view a case in a broader perspective. In the *case* Caton stood silently by while Day increased Caton's wealth, knowing that Day expected him to pay for half the value of the wall when he could have costlessly told Day that he would not make such a payment. In the *hypothetical* (or in one version of the hypothetical) the field owner stood silently by while the laborer increased his wealth, knowing that the laborer expected compensation, when he could have costlessly told the laborer that he would not compensate him. Liability in the hypothetical was more intuitive than liability in the case because in the case Day would benefit from building the wall even if Caton did not pay for half its value, while in the hypothetical the laborer would lose all the value of his labor if the field owner did not compensate him. However, as a matter of social propositions it is hard to see the difference in terms of liability between standing silently by while another increases one's wealth, knowing that the other expects compensation, and standing silently by while another increases one's wealth by his labor while losing the value of his labor if he is not compensated.

In the second form of reasoning from hypotheticals in adjudication a court employs a hypothetical to show, or try to show, that a case should not be decided in a certain way because if the case were decided that way hypothetical similar cases would have to be decided the same way, and deciding those cases the same way would be unsound. This is sometimes referred to as reasoning by slippery slope, the idea being that if the case before the court is decided in a certain way future courts will be required to descend a slippery slope by unsoundly deciding similar cases in the same way.

Slippery slope reasoning is rarely employed in common law cases. For example, with a very minor exception in his article *Slippery Slopes*[4] Frederick Schauer did not cite any common law cases. There are three reasons why slippery-slope arguments are rarely employed in common law cases.

---

[3] *Id.* at 516.
[4] Frederick Schauer, *Slippery Slopes*, 99 HARV. L. REV. 361 (1985).

First, hypothetical slippery slope cases divert the court's attention from the merits of the actual case before it.

Second, hypothetical slippery slope cases are just that – hypothetical – and might never come to pass.

Third, and most important, often or usually hypothetical slippery slope cases are distinguishable from the case before the court, so that a decision in the case would not be determinative in the hypothetical cases even if they did come to pass. This fact is exemplified by *Roberson* v. *Rochester Folding Box Co.*,[5] one of the relatively few common law cases based on slippery slope reasoning. There, Roberson alleged that without her consent Franklin Mills, which was in the business of milling, manufacturing, and selling flour, printed and sold about 25,000 lithographs and photographs of her, above which appeared in large letters "Flour of the Family" and below which appeared in large letters, "Franklin Mills Flour." Roberson sued Franklin on the ground that Franklin had invaded her right of privacy. The New York Court held for Franklin, largely on the basis of a slippery slope argument:

> If [a right to privacy] be incorporated into the body of the law . . . the attempts to logically apply the principle will necessarily result . . . in litigation bordering upon the absurd, for the right of privacy, once established as a legal doctrine, cannot be confined to the restraint of the publication of a likeness but must necessarily embrace as well the publication of a word-picture, a comment upon one's looks, conduct, domestic relations or habits. And were the right of privacy once legally asserted it would necessarily be held to include the same things if spoken instead of printed, for one, as well as the other, invades the right to be absolutely let alone. An insult would certainly be in violation of such a right and with many persons would more seriously wound the feelings than would the publication of their picture, And so we might add to the list of things that are spoken and done day by day which seriously offend the sensibilities of good people to which the principle which the plaintiff seeks to have imbedded in the doctrine of the law would seem to apply.[6]

[5] 171 N.Y. 538 (1902).
[6] *Id.* At 545.

The problem with the Court's reasoning is that many or most of the hypotheticals the court relied upon are easily distinguishable. First, many of the hypotheticals, such as a comment on a person's looks, do not involve an invasion of privacy. Second, the case involved the unauthorized use of a person's portrait for commercial purposes while the hypotheticals did not. And indeed the right of privacy that the Court rejected is today a major body of law.[7]

Reasoning from hypotheticals is also extensively employed in legal education. American law schools teach law in large part through cases. For example, students who study Contracts read cases in casebooks that contain selected contracts cases, and classes are based on a discussion of those cases. Some law school teachers lecture about the cases, but at least in teaching common law subjects many or most law school teachers also or mostly employ the Socratic Method, in which the teacher asks students questions about a case or its holding, rather than lecturing. This Method takes its name from Plato's *Dialogues*, in which Socrates asks another actor a series of probing questions designed to lead the actor to a true understanding of an issue.

The Socratic Method takes two forms, both of which are largely based on hypotheticals.

In one form the teacher asks a series of what-if questions involving hypothetical variations of the facts of a case, as in "Would the result be different if fact X was different?" In the second form, which is more closely based on how Socrates used his method, the teacher asks a series of questions, many based on hypotheticals, which are designed to lead the student to understand the rule that was or should have been applied in the case. Here is an example, drawn from my notes for teaching *Day* v. *Cayton*. (The parentheticals are the answers that I hoped to receive.)

1. [After establishing the facts of the case...] Suppose B goes over to the house of his friend A. When B gets there, A is painting his fence. B starts talking to A, picks up a paintbrush, and helps A to complete

[7] *See* DAN B. DOBBS, DAVID T. HAYDEN & ELLEN M. BUBICK, HORNBOOK ON TORTS 1005–22 (2016); RESTATEMENT OF TORTS sections 652A–652E.

painting the fence. The next day B sends A a bill for his services. Should B recover? (No.)

2. Is there any difference between the hypothetical and *Day* v. *Caton*? (A reasonable person in A's position would not have thought B was expecting payment because he was simply acting as a friend. A reasonable person in Caton's position probably would have thought that Day expected payment.)

3. Why? Did Day lose anything by building the wall on the boundary line? (Yes. Because Day built the wall partly on Caton's land he could not tear the wall down without Caton's agreement.)

4. Did Caton gain anything by the wall? (Yes, the ability to construct a building using the wall as the fourth wall.)

5. Was building the wall on the boundary line then enough to make a reasonable person in Caton's shoes know that the plaintiff expected payment? (Yes.)

6. Is the laborer hypothetical in *Day* v. *Caton* easier or harder than *Day* v. *Caton* itself as regards the issue of whether a reasonable person would think payment was expected? (Easier – the field owner had more reason to know that the laborer's work was being done in expectation of payment because the work benefited only the owner.)

7. Suppose A sends B a written offer to purchase B's 2019 Toyota Camry for $19,000, a fair price. The offer provides that if B does not reject the offer within three days his silence will constitute acceptance. B tears up the offer. Should B be bound? (No.)

8. Why not? Is *Day* v. *Caton* distinguishable from the hypothetical? (A reasonable person in A's position in the Camry hypothetical would not expect that B would be bound by his mere silence, because if B was bound by his silence but didn't want the Camry he would be liable for expectation damages with nothing to show for it. In contrast, in the laborer hypothetical a reasonable person in the laborer's position might expect that the field owner would be bound by his silence because the laborer conferred a substantial benefit on the field owner and would lose the value of his time and labor if the field owner was not bound.)

Finally, reasoning from hypotheticals often plays an important role in oral arguments. In this area slippery-slope reasoning figures prominently, because judges commonly probe counsel with questions along the lines of "If your position is accepted, doesn't A follow?," with A being a result that the judge considers to be demonstrably undesirable.

13 OVERRULING

This Chapter concerns overruling, which occurs when a court over-turns – abolishes – a rule established by binding precedents. Overruling may be explicit or implicit. Explicit overruling occurs when a court explicitly abolishes a rule established by precedents in its jurisdiction and replaces it with the opposite rule. Implicit overruling occurs when a court undoes an established rule but purports not to do so.

At first glance overruling may seem to conflict with the principle of stare decisis. In fact it doesn't, because the principle of stare decisis is subject to various limits, the most important of which is that in most areas of the common law if a rule established in a precedent is not even substantially congruent with social morality and social policy a court may overrule it (see Chapter 3). Furthermore, overruling is governed by an implicit principle found in the case law. This principle reflects three ideals for the common law.

The first ideal is that the body of rules that comprise the common law should be substantially congruent with social morality, social pol-icy, and experience (hereafter "social congruence").

The second ideal is that every rule of the common law should be consistent with every other soundly based rule and should not be subject to inconsistent exceptions.

The third ideal is that common law rules should be relatively stable in order to facilitate planning and protect justified reliance. (The force of this ideal varies by subject-matter. Stability is very important in some areas, such as property, and less important in others, such as torts.) The ideal of stability may conflict with the ideal of social congruence but the likelihood of conflict is reduced because social congruence entails only that a rule be substantially congruent with social propositions, not that it be the best possible rule. Small differences in social congruence are likely to be highly debatable, difficult to determine, or both, so that if the courts were to overturn rules just because they were modestly less socially congruent than competing rules it would be very difficult to replicate legal reasoning or to put much reliance on established rules. Furthermore, the ideal of stability does not conflict with the ideal of social congruence when overruling is foreshadowed, reliance is unjustified, or planning is unlikely.

The overruling principle, which is implicit in the case law is as follows: A common law rule should and normally will be overruled if it is substantially incongruent with social propositions, is inconsistent with other sound rules, has been riddled with inconsistent exceptions, or is manifestly inequitable and unjust, and the value of overruling the rule exceeds the value of retaining it.

EXPLICIT OVERRULING

An example of explicit overruling concerns the charitable immunity doctrine. Under that doctrine a charitable institution is not liable for injuries caused by the negligence of its employees and agents. The major justification proffered for this doctrine was that imposing liability for negligence on a charity would dissipate the charity's assets so that it could no longer carry out its charitable purposes. In its origin an implicit paradigm underlay this justification: that a charitable institution usually was a lone hospital in a small community (most charitable immunity cases concern hospitals) which would not remain economically viable if it was subject to liability for negligence, thereby depriving the members of the community of essential medical services.

At one time the charitable immunity doctrine was the law in most states but today the precedents that established this doctrine have been widely overruled.[1] One reason for the overruling is that the major

---

[1] According to a 1982 Appendix to the Restatement (Second) of Torts, of fifty-three jurisdictions (fifty states, the District of Columbia, Puerto Rico, and the Virgin Islands), thirty-five did not afford immunity to charitable institutions at that time. The Appendix was

proffered justification no longer held, if it ever did. The charitable immunity doctrine may have made some sense when charitable institutions were lone hospitals in small communities and liability insurance was not an established part of conducting an enterprise. However, this justification became unpersuasive when hospitals became large bureaucratic well-funded one-of-many institutions in big cities, and the availability and prevalence of liability insurance made negligence liability an ordinary expense for running such institutions much like salaries and supplies. In addition, the doctrine had become riddled with inconsistent exceptions.

A well-known decision of the United States Court of Appeals for the D.C. Circuit concerning the charitable immunity doctrine is *President and Director of Georgetown College* v. *Hughes*.[2] The defendant in that case was the Georgetown Hospital, a charitable institution. Hughes, a special nurse at the hospital, had been badly injured when a student nurse violently and negligently pushed open a swinging door, which hit Hughes. Hughes sued the hospital, which responded that it was protected by the charitable immunity doctrine.

The court held for Hughes. Six judges participated. The opinion was written by Judge (later Supreme Court Justice) Wiley Rutledge. Three judges, including Rutledge, voted to overturn the charitable immunity doctrine. The other three judges did not write an opinion, but Rutledge wrote that those judges held for Hughes on the ground that her case fell within one of the exceptions to the doctrine. Given the three–three split it could be argued that the court did not overrule the doctrine. However, *Georgetown* is widely regarded as a leading case for overruling the doctrine, and Rutledge's opinion exemplifies the overruling principle.

Rutledge gave four reasons for undoing the charitable immunity doctrine.

First, he dismissed the justification that holding charitable institutions liable for negligence would dissipate an institution's assets so that it could no longer carry out its charitable purposes. Rutledge pointed out that this reason was inconsistent with a major exception to the

---

written almost forty years ago. Given the trend of the law on this issue, it is certain that the number of jurisdictions that do not afford charitable immunity is higher today.
[2] 130 F.2d 810 (D.C. Cir. 1942).

doctrine under which the immunity did not bar suit by "strangers" (persons other than patients), as opposed to beneficiaries (patients). He wrote: "There is ... failure to see [that] dissipation ... [takes] place equally whether damages are paid to a stranger or to a beneficiary of the charity. Damage suits by employees, visitors, special nurses, physicians, and members of the general public are apt to be as frequent and as serious as those by patients."[3]

Second, Rutledge stressed that the exceptions to the charitable immunity doctrine were inconsistent with the doctrine. He singled out the stranger exception:

> No ... tenable foundation [for the exception] exists in considerations of preserving the fund, preventing its dissipation, depriving the intended class or the public of its succor, ... and the like. ... When account is taken of the numbers in both [the stranger and the beneficiary] classes and the probable burden of risk toward each, the heavier risk perhaps is incurred in favor of strangers. ...
>
> If preservation of the fund ... required immunity [it could not justify the stranger distinction]. If the charity can assume the risk as to all the rest of the world and survive, it can do so for those it is designed to help. Neither the number of claims nor their amount will be greater in their behalf than for others. It is probable both would be smaller, because the class is smaller and because it is present in circumstances ordinarily conducive to precaution and care.[4]

(Under another exception, which Rutledge did not address, the charitable immunity doctrine does not apply to "administrative" as opposed to "medical" negligence. In *Bing* v. *Thunig*[5] the New York Court of Appeals said of this exception:

> The hospital contends that the [claimed] negligence occurred during the performance of a "medical" act and, accordingly ..., the doctrine of *respondeat superior* may not be applied to subject it to liability. The difficulty of differentiating between the "medical" and

---

[3] *Id.* at 822.
[4] *Id.* at 826.
[5] 2 N.Y.2d 656 (1957).

the "administrative" in this context ... is thus brought into sharp focus.

That difficulty has long plagued the courts. ... Placing an improperly capped hot water bottle on a patient's body is administrative ... while keeping a hot water bottle too long on a patient's body is medical. ... Administering blood, by means of a transfusion, to the wrong patient is administrative ..., while administering the wrong blood to the right patient is medical .... Employing an improperly sterilized needle for a hypodermic injection is administrative ..., while improperly administering a hypodermic injection is medical .... Failing to place sideboards on a bed after a nurse decided that they were necessary is administrative ..., while failing to decide that sideboards should be used when the need does exist is medical ....[6])

So, Rutledge wrote, "The ... [charitable immunity] rule has pursued an inconsistent course, riddled with numerous exceptions and subjected to various qualifications and refinements."[7]

Third, Rutledge pointed out that because the charitable immunity doctrine applied only to charitable institutions it was inconsistent with the rule that there was no immunity for charitable individuals.

It is a strange distinction, between a charitable institution and a charitable individual, relieving the one and holding the other, for like service and like lapse in like circumstances. The hospital may maim or kill charity patients by negligence, yet the member of its medical staff, operating or attending without pay or the thought of it dare not lapse in a tired or hurried moment.[8]

Fourth, Rutledge pointed out that the charitable immunity doctrine was inconsistent with social morality – specifically, inconsistent with the principle that an actor is morally obliged to act carefully and to compensate persons the actor injures by its negligence. Once it became clear that there was no justification for treating the negligence of a charitable institution differently from the negligence of everyone else it also became clear that as a matter of social morality charitable

---

[6] *Id.* at 663.
[7] *Id.*
[8] *Georgetown* at 814.

institutions were just as morally obliged to act carefully as everyone else.

The charitable immunity doctrine was also inconsistent with experience. As Rutledge wrote:

> No statistical evidence has been presented to show that the mortality or crippling of charities has been greater in states which impose full or partial liability than where complete or substantially full immunity is given. ... Charities seem to survive and increase ..., with little apparent heed to whether they are liable for torts ....
>
> Further, if there is danger of dissipation, insurance is now available to guard against it and prudent management will provide the protection. It is highly doubtful that any substantial charity would be destroyed ... by the cost required to pay the premiums. What is at stake, so far as the charity is concerned, is the cost of reasonable protection, the amount of the insurance premium as an added burden on its finances, not the awarding over in damages of its entire assets.[9]

Rutledge also pointed out that almost all commentators criticized the charitable immunity doctrine. "Scholarly treatment ... is almost uniform. ... [W]hen opinion among scholars ... is uniform or nearly so and that among judges is in high confusion, the former gives direction to the law of the future, while the latter points presently in all directions."[10] Near-unanimous scholarly opinion is important not only because it casts doubt on the soundness of a rule but also because it foreshadows overruling and thereby diminishes the weight to be given to stability.

Rutledge concluded:

> "[T]he rule" has not held in the tests of time and decision. Judged by results, it has been devoured by its "exceptions." Debate has gone on constantly, not so much as to whether but concerning how far it should be "modified" with ever widening modification. ... If we look at results rather than words or forms of statement in opinions for the test of what is the "law" or "the prevailing rule" immunity is not "the rule" and liability "the exception." The rule has become merely a relic in the multitude of departures.[11]

---

[9] *Id.* at 823–24.
[10] *Georgetown* at 812.
[11] *Id.* at 817.

In short, the overruling principle required that the charitable immunity doctrine should be overruled, as it almost universally was. On the one hand, the value of overruling the doctrine was great because the doctrine was substantially incongruent with social morality and experience, was inconsistent with other legal rules that were soundly based, and had been riddled with inconsistent exceptions. On the other hand, the value of retaining the doctrine was small. Reliance, which would principally consist of feeling free to be careless because under the charitable immunity doctrine negligence carried no price, would be unjustified. Planning would not be an issue because due to the availability and widespread use of liability insurance it would be very difficult for a hospital or any other charitable institution to claim that it had not planned for negligence liability. As Rutledge pointed out, the rule had become merely a relic. It was low-hanging fruit, waiting to be picked.[12]

For much the same reasons that led to the overruling of the charitable immunity doctrine, beginning in the 1940s the courts also overruled precedents that established other immunities, such as the school-district immunity,[13] spousal immunity,[14] parental immunity,[15] and the immunity against liability for prenatal injuries.[16] All in all, hundreds of cases overruled various immunities.

Another example of explicit overruling concerns the contributory negligence rule. Under that rule where a plaintiff was injured as a result of the defendant's negligence, but the plaintiff's own negligence contributed to the plaintiff's injury, the plaintiff is barred from recovery (subject to an exception where the defendant had a last clear chance to avoid causing the injury) even if the plaintiff's negligence was slight compared to the defendant's negligence.

Prior to the 1970s this rule had been almost universally adopted in the case law and almost universally condemned by commentators. For

[12] For two more exemplary cases that overruled the charitable immunity doctrine, *see Collopy* v. *Newark Eye and Ear Infirmary*, 27 N.J. 29 (1958) and *Albritton* v. *Neighborhood Centers Ass'n*, 466 N.E. 2d 867 (Ohio 1964).
[13] *See, e.g., Molitor* v. *Kaneland Community Unit District*, 48 Ill.2d 11 (1950).
[14] *See, e.g., Klein* v. *Klein*, 58 Cal.2d 692 (1962).
[15] *See, e.g., Broadbent* v. *Broadbent*, 184 Ariz. 74 (1995); *Woods* v. *Lancet*, 303 N.Y. 349.
[16] *See, e.g., Tucker* v. *Howard L. Carmichael & Sons*, Inc., 208 Ga. 201 (1951); *Amann* v. *Faidy*, 415 Ill. 422 (1953).

example, in their leading *Hornbook on Torts*, Dobbs, Hayden, and
Burbick wrote that the doctrine of contributory negligence "departed
seriously from the ideals of accountability and deterrence because it
completely relieved the defendant from liability even if he was by far the
most negligent actor."[17] Because the contributory negligence rule was
manifestly inequitable and unjust the value of overruling the rule was
great. In contrast, the value of retaining the rule was minimal. The only
way an actor could claim to have relied on the contributory negligence
rule would be to argue that because of the rule the actor was more
careless than otherwise would have been the case, and reliance of this
kind would be unjustified. For the same reason, actors could not
justifiably plan on the basis of the rule.

Because the contributory negligence rule was inequitable and unjust
it has now been universally overturned in favor of the comparative
negligence rule. Under that rule, a plaintiff whose negligence contributed to its injury is not barred from recovery; instead, the recovery is
reduced based on the degree to which the plaintiff's own negligence
contributed to the plaintiff's injury. Much of this overturning was
legislative, but the courts also contributed by overruling the contributory negligence rule, beginning with *Hoffman* v. *Jones*,[18] decided by the
Florida Supreme Court in 1973. There the Court wrote that it was
"unjust and inequitable to vest an entire accidental loss on one of the
parties whose negligence combined with the negligent conduct of the
other party to produce the loss."[19] Two years later, in *Li* v. *Yellow
Cab*,[20] the California Court, in overruling the California precedents
that established the contributory negligence rule, wrote:

> It is unnecessary for us to catalogue the enormous amount of
> critical comment that has been directed over the years against the
> "all-or-nothing" approach of the doctrine of contributory negli-
> gence. The essence of that criticism has been constant and clear:
> the doctrine is inequitable in its operation because it fails to distrib-
> ute responsibility in proportion to fault. Against this have been

[17] DAN B. DOBBS, PAUL T. HAYDEN & ELLEN M. BURBICK, HORNBOOK ON TORTS 380 (2d ed.
2016).
[18] 280 So.2d 431 (1973).
[19] *Id.* at 436.
[20] 532 P.2d 1228 (1975).

raised several arguments in justification, but none have proved even remotely adequate to the task. The basic objection to the doctrine— grounded in the primal concept that in a system in which liability is based on fault, the extent of fault should govern the extent of liability—remains irresistible to reason and all intelligent notions of fairness.[21]

IMPLICIT OVERRULING

If a rule established in a precedent qualifies for overruling under the overruling principle normally courts will overrule it. In some cases, however, instead of explicitly overruling the precedent a court implicitly overrules it by the process of transformation, in which a court purports to follow a precedent while actually undoing it.

Cases involving transformation depart from the principle that the rule established in a precedent is the rule that the precedent court stated determined the result. Instead, a transforming court carves the precedent down to its result, effectively disregards what the precedent court said, and adopts a new rule that it claims is consistent with the precedent although in fact it is not.

For example, in *Sherlock* v. *Stillwater Clinic*,[22] decided in 1977, the Minnesota Supreme Court transformed a rule that the Court had established in *Christensen* v. *Thornby*, decided in 1934.[23] In that case Christensen's wife had experienced great difficulty in giving birth to her first child and was told that it would be dangerous to bear another. Thornby, a physician, advised Christensen that a vasectomy would protect his wife against conception; performed the operation; told Christensen that it had been successful; and guaranteed sterility. The report was incorrect: the vasectomy was not successful. Subsequently

---

[21] *See also, e.g., Battalla* v. *New York*, 10 N.Y. 2d 237, 239 (1961) ("It is our opinion that Mitchell should be overruled. It is undisputed that a rigorous application of the rule would be unjust, as well as opposed to experience and logic."); *Javins* v. *First National Realty Corp.*, 428 F.2d 1021 (D.C. Cir. 1970) (J. Skelly Wright, J.) ("Courts have a duty to reappraise old doctrines in light of the facts and circumstances of contemporary life. . . . As we have said before, '[T]he continued vitality of the common law . . . depends on its ability to reflect community values and ethics.'").

[22] 260 N.W.2d 169 (Minn. 1977).

[23] 192 Minn. 123 (1934).

Mrs. Christensen became pregnant and gave birth. She survived but Christensen sued Thornby to recover for his emotional injury and financial expenses as a result of the pregnancy and birth. The Minnesota Court affirmed a verdict for Thornby on two grounds: first, that Christensen had not alleged that Thornby acted with fraudulent intent; and second, that the birth of a healthy child did not constitute an injury. The court said: "The expenses alleged are incident to the bearing of a child and their avoidance is remote from the avowed purpose of the operation. As well might the plaintiff charge the defendant with the cost of nurture and education of the child through its minority."[24]

Sherlock was strikingly similar to *Christensen*. The Sherlocks had seven children and wanted to ensure that their family would not grow larger. To that end they consulted Dr. Stratte, a member of the Stillwater Clinic, who performed a vasectomy. Two months later, Mr. Sherlock brought a sample of his semen to the Clinic for testing and Dr. Stratte reported that his semen was free of sperm. In reliance on this report the Sherlocks resumed normal sexual relations. The report was incorrect; Mr. Sherlock's semen was not free of sperm. As a result, Mrs. Sherlock became pregnant and gave birth to a healthy baby. The Sherlocks sued the Clinic and Dr. Stratte, requesting damages for Mrs. Sherlock's pain and suffering during pregnancy and delivery, the expense of maintaining and educating the child until the age of majority, and for Mr. Sherlock's temporary loss of his wife's conjugal companionship.

Recall that in *Christensen* the Court said "As well might the plaintiff charge the defendant with the cost of nurture and education of the child through its minority" – exactly what the Sherlocks requested. The court did not overrule *Christensen* but it transformed that case and held that the Sherlocks could recover the damages they sought:

> Apart from the technical disposition [made in *Christensen*] the court in that case expressly held ... that an action, if properly pleaded, could be maintained against a physician for the improper performance of such an operation. Viewed in its proper posture, the

[24] *Id.* at 126.

Christensen case stands solely for the proposition that a cause of action exists for an improperly performed sterilization.[25]

Perhaps the most important example of transformation is *MacPherson* v. *Buick Motor Co.*, decided by the New York Court of Appeals in an opinion by Cardozo, which transformed a rule adopted in a string of New York cases dating back to *Thomas* v. *Winchester*,[26] decided in 1852. Winchester had produced and negligently labeled a jar of belladonna, a poison, as dandelion, a medicine. Thomas bought the jar from a pharmacist, took the belladonna, and became gravely ill. The court held that a negligent manufacturer whose defective product caused an injury was liable only to its immediate buyer, but made an exception where the product put human life in imminent danger and ruled for Thomas on the ground that the jar of belladonna was imminently dangerous.

Thereafter, the New York courts oscillated on whether a given product was or was not imminently dangerous. In *Loop* v. *Litchfield*,[27] decided by the New York Court in 1870, a manufacturer had negligently constructed a circular saw, which flew apart and fatally injured the plaintiff, who had taken possession of the saw from the original buyer. The Court declined to apply the imminent-danger exception and held for the manufacturer. In *Losee* v. *Clute*,[28] decided by the New York Court in 1873, a manufacturer had negligently constructed a steam boiler, which exploded and injured the plaintiff's property. The Court declined to apply the imminent-danger exception and held for the manufacturer. In *Devlin* v. *Smith*,[29] decided by the New York Court in 1882, the defendant had negligently constructed painters' scaffolding, which caused the death of a worker. The Court applied the imminent-danger exception and held the defendant liable. In *Statler* v. *George A. Ray Mfg. Co.*,[30] decided by the New York Court in 1909, the defendant had negligently constructed a restaurant-sized coffee urn, which exploded and injured the plaintiff, who had purchased the

[25] 260 N.W. at 172.
[26] 6 N.Y. 381 (1852).
[27] 42 N.Y. 351 (1870).
[28] 51 N.Y. 494 (1873).
[29] 89 N.Y. 470 (1882).
[30] 195 N.Y. 478 (1909).

urn from a distributor. The Court applied the imminent-danger exception and held for the plaintiff.

This brings us to *MacPherson*. There, Buick Motor Company had manufactured a car that it sold to a dealer who resold it to MacPherson. One of the car's wheels was made of defective wood. The wheel collapsed while MacPherson was driving. He was injured and sued Buick. Buick purchased the wheel from another manufacturer, but there was evidence that a reasonable inspection by Buick would have discovered the defect. MacPherson won a jury verdict against Buick, which appealed. The rule governing a manufacturers liability for negligence fell within the overruling principle because it was inconsistent with the negligence principle and there was no good reason of social morality or social policy why a manufacturer should not be liable for its negligence. But Cardozo did not explicitly overrule it. Instead, he reached the same result by transforming the rule:

> We hold, then, that the principle of *Thomas* v. *Winchester* is not limited to poisons, explosives, and things of like nature, to things which in their normal operation are implements of destruction. If the nature of a thing is such that it is reasonably certain to place life and limb in peril when negligently made, it is then a thing of danger. ... If to the element of danger there is added knowledge that the thing will be used by persons other than the purchaser, and used without new tests, then, irrespective of contract, the manufacturer of this thing of danger is under a duty to make it carefully.[31]

In form, Cardozo did not overrule the cases that adopted the manufacturer's liability rule and the imminent danger exception, but only purported to extend the rule and the exception. In substance, however, Cardozo transformed both the rule and the exception by adopting in their place the rule that "If the nature of a thing is such that it is reasonably liable to place life and limb in peril when negligently made, it is then a thing of danger," and the manufacturer is liable if it made the thing negligently. Under this rule liability no longer turned on whether a thing was imminently dangerous. Instead, liability turned on whether a thing was dangerous if negligently made, and since any good is dangerous if negligently made, under the rule Cardozo adopted

[31] 217 N.Y. at 389.

manufacturers were liable to all persons injured by their negligence, not only to their immediate buyers. To put it differently, Cardozo transformed both the manufacturer's liability rule and the imminent danger exception into a simple negligence rule – the same rule that applies to persons other than manufacturers.

ACKNOWLEDGMENTS

This book benefits from the contributions of many people. Judge Harris Hartz, my long-time colleague Jan Vetter, and Professor Steve Ross read drafts of either the entire book or many chapters and made comments that significantly improved the book. My Dean, Erwin Chemerinsky, read and made extensive and terrific comments on the drafts of every chapter as I wrote them, and most of those comments are reflected in this book. Two anonymous peer reviewers read the final draft and also made extensive and terrific comments, most of which led me to make important revisions in the final manuscript – I wish I could acknowledge them by name. Over the two-year period in which I wrote this book I was assisted first by Toni Mendicino and more recently by Jennifer McBride. Both were and are superb. Edna Lewis, a Reference Librarian at Berkeley Law, consistently provided me with great answers to reference questions, many of which I thought might very well be unanswerable. Montie Magree of Berkeley Law's I.T. Department, provided beyond-belief computer support, as did Ryan Tran. Laura Ventura Moreno, Araly Majano, Paola Gorrostieta, Mary Tan, Mila Carsolo, and Mina Enrique gave me loving support throughout. I could not have written this book without the aid of Toni, Jennifer, Edna, Montie, Ryan, Laura, Araly, Paola, Mary, Mila, and Mina.

INDEX

Garner, Bryan, 16
good judgment, in legal reasoning, 89
Goodhart, Arthur, 25–26
Greenawalt, Kent, 35–36
Gregory v. *Cott*, 54, 56

Hadley v. *Baxendale*, 28–29, 57–58,
     67–69
Hart, H. L. A., 34, 48–49. *See also*
     authoritative rules
  on common law legal rules
     core of, 64, 87–88
     penumbra of, 64, 87–88
  on critical morality, 43
  on legal positivism, 48–51
     reliance principle and, 50
     tenets of, 49–50
     unconscionability principle and, 50
  on social morality, 43–44
Hart, Henry, 27
Hartz, Harris, 15–16
hearsay rule, 74–75
Hector Martinez and Co. v. *Southern Pacific
     Transp. Co.*, 69
Hernandez v. *Hammond Homes, Ltd.*, 5–7
Hindu law, 1
hiving off new legal rules, 71–73
  distinguishing principle compared to,
     80–81
Hoffman v. *Jones*, 58
holdings, 27–29
  Angel v. *Murray*, 28–29
  Hadley v. *Baxendale*, 28–29
horizontal stare decisis, 21–22
  law-of-the-Circuit doctrine, 22
hypotheticals, legal reasoning from
  application of, 90
  Day v. *Caton*, 92–93
  in legal education, 95–97
  slippery slope reasoning, 93–95
     Roberson v. *Rochester Folding Box Co.*,
        94–95
  Vincent v. *Lake Erie Transportation Co.*,
        90–92

implicit overruling, 106–10
  Christensen v. *Thornby*, 106–8
  lack of candor in, 110
  MacPherson v. *Buick Motor Co.*, 108–10
  Sherlock v. *Stillwater Clinic*, 106–8
  Thomas v. *Winchester*, 108–10

inconsistent legal exceptions, 76–78
Islamic law, 1

jurisdictional limits on stare decisis principle,
     23–24

Kaplow, Louis, 63
Kenford Co. v. *Erie County*, 65
Kirksey v. *Kirksey*, 37–38

Lamond, Grant, 82
The Law of Judicial Precedent (Garner),
     16
law-of-the-Circuit doctrine, 22
legal education, hypotheticals in,
     95–97
legal positivism, 48–51
  reliance principle and, 50
  tenets of, 49–50
  unconscionability principle and, 50
legal precedent. *See* precedent
legal principles, 61–63
  legal rules compared to, 62–63
legal reasoning. *See also* common law
     reasoning; rule-based reasoning;
     social morality
  analogy-based, 7–8
     datasets for, 7–8
     limitations of, 8
  empirical positions in, 41–48, 55–57
  by fact analogy, 85
  good judgment as element of, 89
  rule-based
     doctrine of comparative negligence,
        57–58
     Hadley v. *Baxendale*, 57–58
     Hoffman v. *Jones*, 58
     right of privacy, 58–59
  similarity-based, 8–9
  social policy in, 41–48
     contract law and, 44–45
legal rules, in common law, 60–61. *See also*
     rule-based legal reasoning;
     rule-based reasoning; rules
  Contemporary Mission, Inc. v. *Famous
     Music Corp.*, 66–67
  core of, 64, 87–88
  deferred standards compared to, 63
  Hadley v. *Baxendale*,
     67–69
  Hart on, 64, 87–88

For EU product safety concerns, contact us at Calle de José Abascal, 56–1°, 28003 Madrid, Spain or eugpsr@cambridge.org.

www.ingramcontent.com/pod-product-compliance
Ingram Content Group UK Ltd.
Pitfield, Milton Keynes, MK11 3LW, UK
UKHW020351140625
459647UK00020B/2394